DANIEL MOORE

Marriage as a Mission

Living Out God's Design for Marriage

To my wife, Michelle
You are God's greatest gift to me and the heartbeat of this book.
Your love, patience, and unwavering faith have carried me through
seasons I could never have faced alone. Thank you for walking
beside me for more than twenty years, for believing in us when
times were hard, and for showing me daily what it means to love as
Christ loves the church. This book is as much yours as it is mine and
is dedicated to you, my best friend and forever love.

Within this Christian vision for marriage, here's what it means to fall in love. It is to look at another person and get a glimpse of the person God is creating, and to say, 'I see who God is making you, and it excites me! I want to be part of that. I want to partner with you and God in the journey you are taking to his throne. And when we get there, I will look at your magnificence and say, 'I always knew you could be like this. I got glimpses of it on earth, but now look at you!

Timothy Keller

Contents

Preface

Marriage was never meant to be an afterthought or simply a convenient arrangement between two people. From the very beginning, God designed marriage as a covenant, a reflection of His love, and a mission field in itself. Yet in today's culture, the beauty and purpose of marriage often get lost amid selfish desires, broken commitments, and competing voices about what marriage should be.

This book was born out of a deep conviction that marriage is more than just companionship — it is a calling. It is one of the clearest pictures we have of Christ's love for the church, and it carries with it a responsibility to live out that truth daily. My wife, Michelle, and I have been on this journey for over twenty years, learning through joys and challenges alike that marriage is not about perfect spouses, but about a perfect Savior working in and through imperfect people.

Marriage as a Mission is not a manual filled with quick fixes or surface-level advice. Instead, it's an invitation to rediscover God's design for marriage and to embrace the role He intended it to play in our homes, communities, and the world. Along the way, you'll find biblical truths, real-life stories, and practical applications to help you view your marriage as more than just a personal blessing; it's a Kingdom assignment.

My prayer is that as you turn these pages, you'll be reminded that your marriage has eternal significance. Whether you're newlyweds, seasoned spouses, or somewhere in between, may this book encourage you to walk hand in hand, not just with each other, but with the Lord, as you live out your marriage as a mission.

—Daniel Moore

Acknowledgments

First and foremost, I want to thank my Lord and Savior, Jesus Christ. Without Him, this book would have no purpose, and without His grace, I would have no story to tell. Every page is a reflection of His faithfulness.

To my wife, Michelle — thank you for standing by my side for more than twenty years, for loving me through every high and low, and for co-laboring with me in ministry and in life. You are my partner, my encourager, and my best friend.

To my kids and spouses — thank you for teaching me more about love, patience, and joy than I could have ever imagined. To my granddaughters, you are a constant reminder of God's goodness and the blessing of family.

A heartfelt thank you to our dear friends, Scottie and Vicky Albious. Your friendship has been such a blessing in our lives. Thank you for inviting Michelle and me to our very first XO Conference, the spark that began our journey toward complete marriage restoration. Your love for one another, even in your differences, has been an inspiring example to us of what it truly looks like for a couple to walk in unity and love. We are forever grateful for your influence and encouragement.

I am also grateful to my church family, friends, and mentors who have poured into me over the years. Your encouragement and prayers gave me the strength to press forward when this project felt overwhelming.

A special thank you to the listeners of *Connecting the Gap* and *Marriage Life and More.* Your support and feedback inspire me to keep sharing truth and encouragement each week.

Finally, to everyone who picks up this book — thank you. My prayer is that the words within these pages point you to Christ and inspire you to live out God's beautiful design in your life, relationships, and your marriages.

Part 1: God's Blueprint for Marriage

1. The Origin of Marriage: God's Design, Not Man's Idea

L et's be honest — if marriage were a human invention, it would probably look a lot different. For starters, we'd likely have an app for that. You know, something like 'Build-A-Spouse', just swipe left on laziness, upgrade communication skills, and maybe add a 'listen-and-don't-just-nod' feature. Problem solved, right?

But marriage didn't originate in a tech lab or an office board-room. It was God's design from the beginning, before dinner reservations, dual-income debates, or 'pick your honeymoon on Pinterest'. Yet today, many act as if marriage is something we just made up, like a weekend hobby that comes with return policies.

It's like someone buying a Picasso, hanging it sideways, scribbling on it with a marker, and then saying, 'Look at my masterpiece!' That's often how we treat marriage, as if we own it and can rework it however we please. But trying to redesign marriage without the Designer is a bit like trying to rewrite Romeo and Juliet with a happy ending and no Shakespeare — it misses the point entirely.

So the truth is, marriage was God's idea before anyone ever thought it needed a registry or a Pinterest board. Man just keeps trying to claim copyright on a masterpiece only heaven could create.

This book was written to remind us that marriage is more than just a partnership for companionship or happiness here on earth; it was created by God with a greater purpose in mind. From the very beginning, God designed marriage to reflect His covenant love and to be a living picture of Christ and the Church. That means our marriages carry a mission.

This mission is not just about building strong relationships between husband and wife, but about fulfilling God's higher calling: to advance His kingdom, to raise the next generation in faith, and to show the world what His love looks like in action. Every marriage is meant to be a testimony, a ministry, and a tool in God's hands to accomplish His work.

In this book, we will walk through how embracing God's design for marriage transforms the way we live together, love one another, and serve Him. It's about seeing marriage not as an end in itself, but as part of God's greater plan to use us, as couples, for His glory.

Let's get started!

GENESIS 2: GOD'S CREATION OF MARRIAGE

In Genesis 2:18–25, we find God's original design and purpose for marriage. The passage begins with God observing something significant about Adam: he was alone.

Genesis 2:18 says, '*Then the Lord God said, It is not good that the man should be alone; I will make him a helper fit for him.*'

This is the first time in the creation account that God declares something as 'not good.' Up until now, everything God made was declared good or very good. But here, Adam's lack of companionship was not ideal. So God Himself initiates the solution to create a companion who corresponds to him, someone suitable or 'fit' for him.

What follows is not just a moment of companionship being formed, but the first marriage covenant being established. God brings every creature before Adam, but none are found to be a suitable helper. Then in verses 21–22: '*So the Lord God caused a deep sleep to fall upon the man, and while he slept, took one of his ribs and closed up its place with flesh. And the rib that the Lord God had taken from the man, he made into a woman and brought her to the man.*'

Here we see God's direct involvement. He is not just creating a person; He is crafting a relationship. Notice that God brings the woman to Adam, much like a father walks a bride down the aisle. This is not a coincidence; it reflects a divine giving away of the bride.

When Adam sees Eve, he breaks into poetic expression in verse 23: '*Then the man said, This at last is bone of my bones and flesh of my flesh; she shall be called Woman, because she was taken out of Man.*'

This shows a deep recognition, Adam sees in Eve a reflection of himself, yet with a unique and complementary distinction.

Then comes verse 24, the foundational verse for all biblical understanding of marriage: '*Therefore a man shall leave his father and his mother and hold fast to his wife, and they shall become one flesh.*'

This verse sets forth God's purpose and pattern for marriage:

1. **Leaving** - Marriage requires a shift in loyalty and priority. You leave your original family as your primary relational unit.

4

2. **Cleaving (Hold fast)** – This speaks to covenant commitment — a binding together, not a temporary contract.
3. **One flesh** – Points to both physical union and comprehensive unity — emotionally, spiritually, financially, and relationally.

It's worth noting that Jesus Himself quoted Genesis 2:24 in Matthew 19:4–6 when the Pharisees questioned Him about marriage and divorce. He said: *'Have you not read that he who created them from the beginning made them male and female, and said, Therefore a man shall leave his father and his mother and hold fast to his wife, and the two shall become one flesh? So they are no longer two but one flesh. What therefore God has joined together, let not man separate.'*

This confirms God's intention that marriage be a life-long union reflecting unity, covenant love, and divine initiative.

Paul also highlights this in Ephesians 5:31–32, where he again quotes Genesis and then says, *'This mystery is profound, and I am saying that it refers to Christ and the church.'*

So we learn that God's purpose for marriage goes beyond companionship. It serves as a picture of Christ's relationship with His people: sacrificial, loving, enduring, and uniting. The relationship between husband and wife becomes a living parable of a much bigger story — redemption.

Genesis 2 shows us that God created marriage, not man. He designed it for relationship, covenant, and unity, ultimately to reflect His glory, not merely to alleviate loneliness or provide structure to society, but to mirror something eternal and divine. Modern culture may try to redefine marriage, but in the beginning, God defined it with clarity, beauty, and purpose.

MARRIAGE AS COVENANT, NOT CONTRACT

Marriage is, biblically, a covenant, not a contract, and the differ-ence between the two is not only essential but also foundational for Christian couples to understand. While a contract is a mutual agreement based on performance and conditions, a covenant is a sacred, binding promise rooted in faithfulness, love, and lifelong commitment, not just to one another, but to God as well.

A contract says, 'If you do your part, I'll do mine.' It's based on mutual benefit and can break down when one party fails to uphold their end of the agreement. In contrast, a covenant says, 'I will remain faithful regardless of your actions.' A covenant is not dependent on circumstances or emotions; it is a solemn vow that involves both vertical (to God) and horizontal (to spouse) commitments.

The concept of marriage as a covenant is supported through-out Scripture.

Malachi 2:14 says: *'Because the Lord was witness between you and the wife of your youth, to whom you have been faithless, though she is your companion and your wife by covenant.'*

Here, God explicitly calls marriage a covenant. And more than that, He declares that He Himself is a witness to the union. This means that marriage isn't merely a human arrangement; it takes place in the sight of God, and He takes it seriously.

Another example is found in Proverbs 2:16-17, where the adulterous woman is described as someone who: *'...forsakes the companion of her youth and forgets the covenant of her God.'*

Again, the marital bond is described as a covenant, not just between two people, but with God Himself included.

Ezekiel 16:8 also uses covenantal language in describing God's

6

relationship with His people as one of deep matrimonial love: *'I made my vow to you and entered into a covenant with you, declares the Lord God, and you became mine.'*

This shows that the biblical covenant is deeply relational, intimate, and steadfast — not merely transactional or legal.

In the New Testament, Jesus echoes and reinforces this understanding in Matthew 19:5-6: *'Therefore a man shall leave his father and his mother and hold fast to his wife, and the two shall become one flesh. So they are no longer two but one flesh. What therefore God has joined together, let not man separate.'*

By using the language of 'joined together' and 'one flesh,' Jesus lifts marriage beyond a simple social construct to a divine joining, something only God can rightfully separate.

Paul picks up the same imagery in Ephesians 5:25 when he calls husbands to love their wives: *'Husbands, love your wives, as Christ loved the church and gave himself up for her.'*

This verse shows the selfless, sacrificial nature of covenant love. Christ didn't wait until the church was perfect. He initiated love, committed Himself, and remained faithful through suffering and sacrifice. That's a covenant.

When couples see marriage as a contract, it's easy to walk away if things get difficult or if the emotional or material returns decline. But when they see it as a covenant, made before God and patterned after Christ's love, they understand that it is a sacred promise to be honored, protected, and nurtured, even through trials.

Understanding marriage as a covenant helps Christian couples anchor their relationship in eternal truth rather than in temporary feelings. It calls them to higher faithfulness, deeper love, and greater perseverance, knowing that God Himself is involved in their union.

7

WHY GOD DESIGNED IT AS A REFLECTION OF HIS IMAGE

God designed marriage as a reflection of His image, and this divine intention is woven into the very fabric of creation. In Genesis 1:26-27, we see that human beings were made in the image of God: *'Then God said, Let us make man in our image, after our likeness... So God created man in his own image, in the image of God he created him; male and female he created them.'*

This passage tells us two essential truths. First, humanity bears the image of God. Second, this image-bearing is expressed through both males and females. The fact that God created humanity in two complementary sexes, both bearing His image, tells us that relationship, unity, and diversity are part of what it means to reflect God.

God Himself exists in perfect relational unity as a triune being, Father, Son, and Holy Spirit. Marriage, therefore, reflects this relational nature of God, especially in the way two distinct individuals become one flesh (Genesis 2:24). It models unity within diversity, self-giving love, and mutual submission, characteristics that mirror the community and love within the Trinity.

Paul clarifies this even more in Ephesians 5:31-32, where he says: *'Therefore a man shall leave his father and mother and hold fast to his wife, and the two shall become one flesh. This mystery is profound, and I am saying that it refers to Christ and the church.'*

Here, Paul reveals that marriage was always meant to point beyond itself to the ultimate love story, the union between Christ and His church. This means that every Christian marriage is not just a union between husband and wife, but a living parable of how Jesus loves, serves, and commits to His people.

This understanding has deep implications for our marriages

today:

1. **Our marriages are about more than us.** They are designed to reflect God's character and tell His story. Love, grace, forgiveness, and faithfulness in marriage point others to the gospel.
2. **Marriage should be marked by sacrificial love.** Ephesians 5:25 commands, 'Husbands, love your wives, as Christ loved the church and gave himself up for her.' This sets a high standard; our love in marriage is not based on feelings or convenience, but on Christ's example of selfless sacrifice.
3. **Marriage models unity and equality in distinction.** Just as the Father, Son, and Spirit are equally God yet have distinct yet complementary roles, so marriage reflects a divine unity between two individuals who are distinct yet complementary.
4. **Our marriages reflect God's covenant faithfulness.** As God remains faithful to His people despite their flaws, spouses are called to stay loyal to one another. Hosea's story puts this on full display; his relationship with his unfaithful wife mirrors God's relentless love for Israel.

In short, God designed marriage not only for companionship, procreation, or societal stability, but primarily to reflect His own image and love. When Christian couples view marriage this way, it inspires humility, purpose, and a pursuit of holiness. We begin to see our marriages not just as personal relationships, but as sacred spaces where the glory of God is put on display for the world to see.

Marriage as a Mission – Reflection & Action Guide
Reflection Questions

1. Do you tend to see marriage as a contract or a covenant? Why?
2. How has your spouse helped you reflect God's image more fully?
3. What cultural lies about marriage have influenced your expectations?

Mission in Action

- Read Genesis 2:18–25 together.
- Write a short "marriage covenant statement" (2–3 sentences).
- Pray together, surrendering your marriage back to God.

2. The Gospel in Marriage

They say marriage is a lot like a mirror — you quickly start to see the real you, flaws and all. And if you're anything like me, you start wondering why that mirror seems to exaggerate your messier moments and whisper them louder when your spouse is nearby. But here's the twist: that's precisely where the beauty of the gospel shines brightest.

Marriage isn't just about two imperfect people trying to live under one roof; it's about two people learning to give grace daily, just as they've received it. Think of it as the joyful (and sometimes bumpy) journey of sanctification with your favorite roommate, best friend, and occasional sheet-stealer. Marriage, in God's design, isn't just about happiness; it's about holiness. And nothing shows us the depth of God's love quite like a dirty dish argument that ends with, 'I forgive you.'

Let's explore how the gospel shapes our marriages, not just in significant theological ways, but in the laughter, the learning, and yes, even the laundry!

EPHESIANS 5: CHRIST AND THE CHURCH AS A MODEL

In Ephesians 5:22-33, the Apostle Paul presents one of the most beautiful pictures of marriage found in all of Scripture. At first glance, it might seem like Paul is simply giving practical advice to husbands and wives. But a closer look reveals he's doing something far deeper; he's connecting the mystery of marriage directly to the gospel.

Paul writes, *'Wives, submit to your own husbands, as to the Lord... Husbands, love your wives, as Christ loved the church and gave himself up for her.'* That last part, *'as Christ loved the church,'* is the anchor point for understanding marriage through the gospel lens. Marriage, in God's design, isn't just a social contract or even just a loving partnership. It is intended to be a living portrait of Christ's covenant relationship with His bride, the Church.

When Christ gave Himself up for the church, He didn't do it because the church had earned it or was easy to love. Romans 5:8 reminds us that *'God shows his love for us in that while we were still sinners, Christ died for us.'* That's grace in motion. Every time a spouse chooses to forgive an offense rather than hold a grudge, they're echoing that very same grace. Every act of selfless love, patience, and servant-heartedness in marriage is an opportunity to model the gospel.

Paul continues in Ephesians 5:26-27, saying that Christ's aim was *'to sanctify her, having cleansed her by the washing of water with the word, so that he might present the church to himself in splendor.'* Similarly, godly marriage involves both spouses seeking each other's spiritual good. It's not just about shared bank accounts and family vacations; it's about helping each other grow into the image of Christ.

Look at Philippians 2:5-8, where we see the humility of Christ, that though He was in the form of God, He did not count equality with God a thing to be grasped, but emptied Himself. That kind of humility is necessary in marriage. It means laying down our pride, our preferences, and sometimes our desire to have the last word. You're not trying to win an argument; you're trying to win your spouse's heart by being Christ to them.

1 Corinthians 13, often quoted at weddings, isn't just poetic filler. It's a practical road map for gospel-infused love. *'Love is patient and kind... it does not insist on its own way... it bears all things, believes all things, hopes all things, endures all things.'* That's not natural love—that's supernatural love. The kind rooted in what God has done for us in Christ.

So, when we view marriage through the lens of the gospel, we realize it's not just about our happiness, though joy certainly comes, but about displaying God's covenantal faithfulness to the world. Marriage becomes a mission, a daily opportunity to reflect Christ and His Church in the midst of life's messiness.

And sometimes, that's even in the messiness of laundry piles, burnt dinners, and disagreements about how to load the dishwasher! Those everyday moments are the training ground for gospel love. It's there, often in the smallest acts, that Christ is made visible.

Let's look at an example of how this would play out in a marriage relationship.

Mike and Jenna have been married for five years. They love each other deeply, but like most couples, they have their moments. One evening, Jenna comes home exhausted after a chaotic day at work. The house is a wreck, dinner still needs cooking, and worst of all, Mike, who said he'd be home early to help, walks in an hour late, with a coffee in hand and no apology.

Jenna is frustrated. She wants to let him have it. Her natural instinct is to point out how inconsiderate he's been. Meanwhile, Mike is already tense from a stressful meeting at work. He's defensive and tired. The stage is set for a classic blow-up, hurt feelings, harsh words, and two wounded hearts cold-shouldering each other all evening.

But instead of reacting in frustration, Jenna pauses. She remembers how Christ responded to her when she was undeserving, how He gave grace, not condemnation. So, even though she's upset, she calmly expresses her disappointment, but also says, 'I know you've had a long day. I just really needed you. Can we talk about how we can do this better together?'

Mike, instead of defending himself, remembers that Christ, being God, humbled Himself and served. Philippians 2 runs through his mind, and he realizes he's been putting himself first. So, instead of excusing his behavior, he apologizes sincerely. Not just to smooth things over, but because he wants to love Jenna the way Christ loves the church, sacrificially, humbly, faithfully.

In that moment, something powerful happens. The gospel shapes their reaction. Forgiveness is given. Humility is shown. Instead of a wedge being driven deeper, the heart of Christ pulls them closer together.

That's the gospel in marriage. Not perfection, but persistent grace. Not a scorecard, but sacrificial love. It's knowing that even when one of you fails, and you will, the hope isn't in your performance, but in Christ, who is working in both of you. Daily, in moments like this, marriage becomes more than companionship; it becomes a living, breathing picture of redemption.

MARRIAGE AS A LIVING PARABLE OF REDEMPTION

That brings us to the next point. Marriage as a Living Example of Redemption.

At its core, redemption is a story of love pursuing the un-worthy, rescuing the broken, and restoring the undeserving. That is precisely what God did for us through Christ, and that is exactly what marriage is designed to reflect. The relationship between husband and wife is not just about companionship or romance; it is a daily, tangible picture of the redeeming love of Jesus Christ for His Bride, the Church.

Ephesians 5:25-27 says, '*Husbands, love your wives, as Christ loved the church and gave himself up for her, that he might sanctify her, having cleansed her by the washing of water with the word, so that he might present the church to himself in splendor, without spot or wrinkle or any such thing, that she might be holy and without blemish.*'

This is redemption in action. Christ gave Himself up, a willing, sacrificial act driven not by what we deserved but by His boundless love. His love doesn't just forgive; it transforms. He washes, sanctifies, and restores. In a gospel-shaped marriage, husbands and wives are called to display that same self-giving, restorative love toward each other.

Redemption isn't merely a one-time act; it's a continual process. In marriage, this is clearly seen: when offenses come (and they will), spouses are given opportunities to forgive, not because they deserve it, but because Christ has already forgiven us. Colossians 3:13 says, '*...bearing with one another and, if one has a complaint against another, forgiving each other; as the Lord has forgiven you, so you also must forgive.*'

Think of a husband who deeply wounds his wife with careless words. Perhaps he speaks out of anger, criticism, or neglect. Under normal circumstances, such wounds could grow into bitterness, distance, and isolation. But suppose the wife, though deeply hurt, chooses to address the issue with humility and offers genuine forgiveness, pointing to what Christ has already done. In that case, that relationship takes on the tone of Calvary. Her forgiveness mirrors the forgiveness God offers us, not withholding mercy, but extending it freely, even at personal cost.

Of course, this goes both ways. Redemption in marriage also shows up when a spouse pleads for forgiveness and doesn't meet defense or punishment but receives gentle restoration. Galatians 6:1 says, '*Brothers, if anyone is caught in any transgression, you who are spiritual should restore him in a spirit of gentleness.*'

Restoration, not rejection. Gentleness, not gloating. That's what redemption does.

Redeeming love is not blind to faults, but it chooses to see the other person not through the lens of their worst day, but through the lens of God's grace and redemptive purpose. Jesus said of the woman caught in adultery, '*Neither do I condemn you; go, and from now on sin no more*' (John 8:11). He did not excuse her sin, but He also didn't reject her. He offered a new path, a path of restoration.

Marriage offers these same moments again and again. Like the love story of Hosea and Gomer, a prophet relentlessly pursuing his unfaithful wife, God's love is unyielding and persistent. Hosea 3:1 says, '*And the Lord said to me, "Go again, love a woman who is loved by another man and is an adulteress, even as the Lord loves the children of Israel..."*'

What a picture of redemptive love! Marriage gives us a chance to mirror that kind of love, especially in difficult seasons. Not love based on performance, but a covenantal love grounded in God's faithfulness.

Redemption also involves time — sanctification is a process.

Just as the Church is being sanctified to be presented in splendor, so too husbands and wives walk together through triumphs and failures, joys and valleys, helping each other become more like Christ. 2 Corinthians 3:18 says, '*And we all, with unveiled face, beholding the glory of the Lord, are being transformed into the same image from one degree of glory to another...*'

That transformation process is lived out day by day in a marriage rooted in grace. When a husband and wife remain faithful, even when emotions drift, that too is redemptive. It tells the world: Our love is not based merely on momentary feelings, but on a covenant secured by God's faithfulness.

Take, for example, a couple navigating a season of infertility. Their prayers seem unanswered, there's emotional pain, and even strain between them. Yet they continue to hold each other close, cry together, pray together, and speak God's promises over each other's lives. Every moment they choose not to turn against each other or blame, but instead lean into Christ, they testify to a deeper kind of love, a love that redeems brokenness with hope.

In the end, marriage is not primarily about two people finding happiness, though joy is undoubtedly part of it. At its highest purpose, marriage is about displaying the gospel and making the redemptive love of Christ visible in ordinary life. When both husband and wife urgently pursue reconciliation the way God pursued us, when they choose grace over revenge, patience over pride, humility over entitlement, they proclaim to the world that God is still in the business of redeeming broken things.

And that is a mission worth giving your whole life to.

LOVE, SACRIFICE, SUBMISSION, AND GRACE

Modeling the gospel in marriage involves reflecting Christ's love, sacrifice, submission, and grace within the relationship. Each of these components mirrors the relationship between Christ and the Church and offers a practical way for couples to live out their faith daily.

Love: Love is foundational in marriage, just as it is central to the gospel. Ephesians 5:25 tells husbands, *'Husbands, love your wives, just as Christ loved the church and gave himself up for her.'* This kind of love is selfless and servant-hearted. It's not based on feelings alone, but is grounded in a commitment to seeking the best for the other person.

In 1 Corinthians 13:4–7, Paul describes love as patient and kind, not boastful or proud, not self-seeking or easily angered. Modeling gospel love means embodying these traits, bearing with one another, forgiving faults, and celebrating truth. This type of love points back to Christ's unconditional love for us.

Sacrifice: The gospel is the ultimate picture of sacrifice, Jesus giving Himself for our salvation. This translates into marriage, where both spouses prioritize the other's needs over their own. Philippians 2:3–4 says, *'Do nothing out of selfish ambition or vain conceit. Rather, in humility value others above yourselves, not looking to your own interests but each of you to the interests of the others.'*

In marriage, sacrifice may look like giving up personal preferences for the relationship's unity, placing your spouse's encouragement and growth above your own convenience, and being willing to serve even when it's not reciprocated.

Submission: Submission in the gospel context speaks of voluntary yielding out of love and respect. Ephesians 5:21 commands, *'Submit to one another out of reverence for Christ.'* This mutual submission emphasizes that both the husband and wife are to have a servant attitude.

Ephesians 5:22–24 then outlines how wives are to submit to their husbands as to the Lord, and husbands are to lead their wives lovingly. This doesn't imply inferiority but represents functional roles that emulate Christ and the Church. Jesus Himself submitted to the Father's will (Luke 22:42), showing that submission is honorable and part of godly order.

Grace: In marriage, grace reflects the gospel message of forgiveness, patience, and unmerited kindness. Just as God extends grace toward us despite our failures (Romans 5:8), spouses model the gospel by forgiving offenses and choosing mercy over judgment.

Colossians 3:13 says, *'Bear with each other and forgive one another if any of you has a grievance against someone. Forgive as the Lord forgave you.'* This emphasizes that grace is not earned, it's granted. Practicing grace in marriage builds a relationship rooted in the same mercy that God has shown us, making room for healing and restoration.

When all these aspects, love, sacrifice, submission, and grace, are practiced in marriage, they create a living testimony of the gospel. The marriage then becomes a portrait of Christ's relationship with His people, glorifying God and drawing others to the beauty of His design.

Marriage as a Mission – Reflection & Action Guide
  Reflection Questions

19

1. What part of Christ's love (sacrifice, forgiveness, grace) do you struggle most to mirror in your marriage?
2. How does your relationship display (or fail to display) the gospel to others?
3. When was the last time your spouse's love helped you better understand God's love?

Mission in Action

- Memorize Ephesians 5:25 or 5:33 together.
- Write down one way you can love your spouse this week that reflects Christ's love.
- Share with each other one area you need grace, and pray specifically for that.

3. Marriage as Kingdom Partnership

L et's be real for a second — marriage is more than just two people sharing a closet and arguing about thermostat settings. If that were all it was, we'd all be experts by now! But God had something much more powerful in mind when He created marriage. At its core, it's not just about companionship, comfort, or even cute Instagram couples' photos (though those are fun). Marriage, from a Kingdom perspective, is a partnership with a purpose; it's teamwork on a divine assignment. Think of it like a mission from heaven where love meets leadership... and maybe a few dishes that still need washing!

When two people say 'I do' in the eyes of God, they're not just signing up for a lifetime subscription to each other's quirks and Netflix recommendations. They're enrolling in a divine internship. Marriage becomes an arena where two people sharpen each other, grow together, and reflect God's glory to the world. The Kingdom doesn't need more cute couples; it needs powerful partnerships forged in faith and driven by purpose.

Sure, learning how to work in tandem with someone who insists the towels be folded a certain way might not feel like holy work. But don't underestimate how God uses the everyday grind to build His extraordinary kingdom. Marriage done God's way isn't about two individuals pushing their own agendas; it's about becoming one to push His. It's less about 'me and you' and more about 'us for Him.'

Let's unpack what it really means to operate as a Kingdom-focused couple, without spinning into theological rocket science. We'll look at how purpose and partnership go hand in hand and how marriage, when aligned with God's mission, becomes one of the most transformational forces on earth. Buckle up! This isn't going to be your average love story!

MOVING BEYOND PERSONAL HAPPINESS TO KINGDOM IM-PACT

One of the most crucial shifts we have to make in marriage is moving from the pursuit of personal happiness to the pursuit of Kingdom impact. Now, don't get me wrong, God is not against your happiness. He's not sitting in heaven scowling every time you and your spouse smile on date night. But here's the truth: many of us don't learn until marriage gets real that happiness is a byproduct of Kingdom purpose, not the ultimate goal. If we treat our spouse like a happiness vending machine, pressing buttons and expecting snacks of affirmation, comfort, and unlimited foot rubs, we're setting ourselves up for unmet expectations and serious marital hangry-ness!

Jesus said in Matthew 6:33, 'But seek first the kingdom of God and his righteousness, and all these things will be added to you.' That includes the things we think we want in marriage, peace, joy, and satisfaction, but they come after we've prioritized His purpose. The problem shows up when we start asking, 'Is this making me happy?' instead of, 'Is this bringing God glory and advancing His Kingdom?' One of those questions leads to shallow waters; the other leads to transformation. Kingdom impact will require some spiritual muscle, and yes, sometimes less personal comfort.

Let me give you an example. Imagine your marriage like a rowing boat. If both of you are rowing your own direction, trying to reach your personal islands of happiness, one island has 'Unlimited Shopping', the other has 'Football and Silence', you're going in circles. But when both of you row together toward Heaven's purpose, even if that means passing by your favorite island, you actually get somewhere that matters. Philippians 2:4 reminds us, *'Let each of you look not only to his own interests, but also to the interests of others.'* What if your spouse's growth, calling, and Christ-likeness mattered to you more than your own temporary comfort? Now we're really rowing!

Even Jesus modeled this mindset. In the garden of Gethsemane, He didn't pray, 'Father, let me just do what feels good right now.' He said, 'Not as I will, but as you will' (Matthew 26:39). If our marriages are meant to reflect Christ and the Church (Ephesians 5:25-27), then sacrifice isn't the exception — it's the assignment. That might mean showing grace instead of keeping score, choosing to pray instead of pouting, or serving when you'd rather watch Netflix and disappear under a blanket. But here's the Kingdom secret: when we stop chasing our own happiness and start pursuing God's heart together, He gives us joy that happiness could never match. That's marriage with impact. And yes, that's worth rowing for!

Here's the beautiful irony of the Kingdom of God: the very thing we spend all our energy trying to find, personal happiness, is often waiting for us on the other side of surrender. When we make it our sole focus, it stays just out of reach. But when we choose to seek Kingdom impact first, especially in our marriages, we find ourselves stumbling into a more profound joy than we ever imagined possible. Why? Because happiness in Christ isn't something we chase, it's something we inherit when we align our lives with His purposes.

Psalm 16:11 gives us a strong dose of truth in this area: *'You make known to me the path of life; in your presence there is fullness of joy; at your right hand are pleasures forevermore.'* Fullness of joy, authentic, satisfying, soul-deep joy, is found in His presence, not in perfect circumstances or a 'perfect' spouse. That means a marriage centered on Kingdom purpose will always produce more emotional and spiritual fulfillment than one driven by self-centered priorities. When we let our marriages revolve around God's mission rather than our own preferences, we discover that He takes care of our needs, including our joy.

Too often, we treat happiness like a destination on a GPS. We plug it into our life's navigation system and try to find the fastest route there, hoping marriage, or a spouse, or the next promotion will lead us straight to it. But Jesus said in John 15:11, *'These things I have spoken to you, that my joy may be in you, and that your joy may be full.'* Joy comes from abiding in Him, not arriving at some imaginary life milestone. So if we focus on building a marriage that's rooted in Christ, committed to serving, loving, and growing for His glory, then joy, real joy, shows up as part of the journey.

The truth is, Kingdom living doesn't require us to sacrifice happiness; it just redefines it. It upgrades our understanding from temporary pleasures to eternal fulfillment. And the best news? A marriage lived for Kingdom impact doesn't just bless the two people in it. It overflows, touches others, and leaves a legacy. That's the kind of joy we were created for. Not the kind that fades with mood swings or unmet expectations, but the kind that gets stronger the more we live for Jesus, together.

UNITY WITH PURPOSE: SERVING GOD TOGETHER

When it comes to marriage, unity isn't just about tolerating your spouse's suspicious pasta attempts or agreeing on which way the toilet paper should roll (although, let's face it, that last one is universally over)! Biblical unity goes much deeper; it's about moving together toward a shared purpose: serving God as a team.

Think of marriage like being two oxen yoked together (Deuteronomy 22:10 excluded — we're not saying you're mismatched animals here)! When yoked together correctly, they plow in the same direction, bearing the weight equally. But if one wants to head left and the other to Chick-fil-A, things quickly go sideways. Ephesians 5:21 wisely reminds us to submit to one another out of reverence for Christ. That mutual submission becomes the basis of a powerful, unified team with heavenly purpose.

Ecclesiastes 4:9-12 really drives this home, *'Two are better than one, because they have a good return for their labor.'* It's not just about working better together in tasks like unloading groceries, but about pursuing kingdom goals side by side. Whether you're reaching out to your neighbors, serving in your church, or simply raising your children with godly values, your shared mission strengthens your bond.

In Philippians 2:2, Paul urges believers to be *'like-minded, having the same love, being one in spirit and purpose.'* Now apply that to marriage: if you're both passionate about loving God and loving others, suddenly you're not just roommates, you're co-laborers in Christ. You're aiming your lives not at each other with arguments and annoyances, but ahead, with God as your guiding purpose.

A little humor helps, too. The goal is to bless others; who cares what flavor gets made? That's unity with purpose: laying aside petty preferences for God's bigger picture.

In the end, when couples chase God together, miracles happen. They develop patience, not just because they've learned to let their spouse load the dishwasher 'wrong,' but because they're growing in the fruit of the Spirit (Galatians 5:22-23). They grow in compassion because rubbing shoulders in ministry reveals each other's strengths and weaknesses, and they learn to cover them in love (1 Peter 4:8).

Unity with purpose doesn't mean being identical; it means being intentional. Complementary, not clones. A great duet, not a soloist, and someone shouting from the back row. So take your spouse's hand, not just romantically, but in mission, and serve God together like the powerful, God-designed team you were meant to be. And maybe, just maybe, let them pick the flavor this time!

BIBLICAL COUPLES AS EXAMPLES

Priscilla and Aquila are among the most powerful and inspiring examples of a married couple united by a Kingdom purpose. Their story appears throughout the New Testament, sprinkled like breadcrumbs that together paint a picture of a couple deeply committed to working together for God's mission. They weren't just attendees in the early church; they were workers, leaders, mentors, and missionaries.

Let's begin in Acts 18:1-3: '*After this, Paul left Athens and went to Corinth. And he found a Jew named Aquila, a native of Pontus, recently come from Italy with his wife Priscilla... And because he was of the same trade, he stayed with them and worked, for they were tent makers by trade.'*

Here, we see that Priscilla and Aquila were business owners, tent makers, who opened not just their home but their hearts and their lives to ministry. Paul lived and worked alongside them, likely discipling them while they shared meals, jokes, prayers, and thread.

This wasn't simply about making tents; it was about building the Church. Their home was, in effect, a ministry hub, a launching pad for Kingdom work. Later in Romans 16:3-4, Paul writes: *'Greet Prisca and Aquila, my fellow workers in Christ Jesus, who risked their necks for my life, to whom not only I give thanks but all the churches of the Gentiles give thanks as well.'*

Let that sink in. Not only were they hard at work for Christ, but they were brave enough to put their lives on the line for someone else's ministry. This is a married couple with a unified Kingdom purpose. Priscilla and Aquila didn't argue about whether they had time for ministry; they made time. And it wasn't just Aquila leading while Priscilla fetched coffee; she was mentioned either before or with him in every passage they appear. This suggests an equal partnership in purpose, something remarkably counter-cultural at the time.

One of their most significant joint contributions comes later in Acts 18:24-26: *'Now a Jew named Apollos... came to Ephesus. He was an eloquent man, competent in the Scriptures... He began to speak boldly in the synagogue, but when Priscilla and Aquila heard him, they took him aside and explained to him the way of God more accurately.'*

Apollos was gifted, but needed instruction, and instead of

publicly correcting him or letting his teaching mislead others, this dynamic couple gently pulled him aside and mentored him together. That's discipleship. That's Kingdom work. That's marital unity in action. Imagine the impact: the man they discipled would later become a significant leader in the early church (see 1 Corinthians 3:5-6).

Now, what if Priscilla and Aquila had refused to live with Kingdom purpose? What if they'd said, 'We love God, but really, running a business is enough, and we're just too busy for all this hosting and mentoring.' Imagine Paul arriving in Corinth and being turned away like a door-to-door salesman. No safe place to work, no fellowship, no hospitality. What if young Apollos never got that gentle correction? He might have continued preaching an incomplete gospel, perhaps causing division or confusion in the Body.

Even Apostle Paul hints at the critical nature of these partnerships in 1 Corinthians 3:6: *'I planted, Apollos watered, but God gave the growth.'*

That 'watering' might never have been as effective if it weren't for Priscilla and Aquila's timely role in Apollos's development. That's what their marriage looked like: lives woven tightly together, pulling in the same direction with purpose.

When couples unite around a shared mission for the Kingdom, their impact multiplies exponentially. Think of it like a well-synchronized rowing team; if one spouse goes forward while the other goes backward, they go nowhere fast (and probably get wet). But a unified direction? That turns a simple two-person boat into a vessel God can use to bring others safely across stormy waters.

Priscilla and Aquila weren't preachers in the spotlight or miracle-workers with dramatic stories. They were faithful,

28

humble, and intentional. A married couple who lived out Romans 12:11-13: *'Do not be slothful in zeal, be fervent in spirit, serve the Lord... Contribute to the needs of the saints and seek to show hospitality.'*

That's the vision: service rooted in love, partnership saturated with purpose, and a marriage that doesn't just journey side-by-side but is laser-focused on God's mission.

So, whether you're mentoring future leaders or just inviting someone over for dinner and prayer, remember: sometimes the most powerful ministry begins around the kitchen table with two hearts beating for the same eternal cause. And yes, you can serve kingdom purpose AND have matching coffee mugs. That's called divine efficiency!

Abraham and Sarah are another excellent example of a married couple working together in unity for a Kingdom purpose, though at times with stumbles, doubts, and a few laughs along the way (Genesis 18:12 being a prime example, when Sarah laughs at the idea of having a baby in her 90s).

God called Abraham in Genesis 12:1-3 to leave his country, his kindred, and his father's house, with a promise to make him a great nation. Although the call specifically came to Abraham, it required Sarah's full participation. She left behind all familiarity, embracing a nomadic life filled with tents, uncertainty, and the occasional awkward family moment, such as nearly being taken into royal harems not once but twice (Genesis 12:14-20; 20:1-18). Talk about needing strong marital trust!

Sarah's role wasn't just passive. Hebrews 11:11 honors her saying, *'By faith Sarah herself received power to conceive, even when she was past the age, since she considered him faithful who had promised.'* Though she laughed at first, she later came to

29

believe. And together, Abraham and Sarah brought forth Isaac, the child of promise, through whom God's covenant line would continue.

Imagine if Sarah had refused to go with Abraham in Genesis 12. Suppose she'd said, *'You go, Abe. I'm staying here with the family and the stable plumbing.'* Without her support, courage, and eventual faith, the story of God's covenant people would have looked drastically different.

What makes their partnership powerful is their shared endurance through long periods of waiting, their journey through faith and failure, and their commitment to following God's direction despite not having all the answers in advance. Romans 4:19 says that Abraham did not weaken in faith, even when he considered his and Sarah's old age, showing that their spiritual unity went beyond human logic.

Their life illustrates that serving God together as a married couple doesn't require perfection; it requires faith. There will be delays, detours, and moments of doubt, but a shared vision of God's promises can sustain marriage and transform history.

In modern-day terms, it's like signing up for a lifelong road trip with no GPS, no timeline, and only God's promise that it leads to blessing. Sarah wasn't just in the passenger seat; she was a co-pilgrim of faith. Their journey shows us that when couples dare to trust God together, even their barrenness can become a birthing ground for God's most significant work: birthing a kingdom partnership.

Marriage as a Mission – Reflection & Action Guide
Reflection Questions

1. How has God uniquely gifted you as individuals and as a

couple?

2. Do you currently see your marriage as serving a kingdom purpose, or more as a means of survival?

3. What would it look like to align your marriage with God's mission?

Mission in Action

- Make a list of 3 ways you could serve God better together than apart.
- Pray for wisdom about one ministry or mission you can commit to as a couple.
- Share with one another where you sense God is calling your partnership forward.

Part 2: Building a God-Centered Marriage

4. Christ at the Center

I t's easy to believe that love, and by extension, marriage, is powered by roses, butterflies, and just the right Spotify playlist. But the truth is, while those things are nice (and yes, playlists matter), they won't keep a marriage on course when life throws in-laws, laundry, and late-night arguments about thermostat settings your way. Enter the idea of putting God at the center, because if you're going to build something as ambitious and beautiful as marriage, wouldn't it make sense to consult the Architect?

At the heart of this chapter is a simple but powerful idea: marriage works best when it's not just between two people, but among three, husband, wife, and God. It's like a triangle. Not the scary kind from high school geometry class, but the kind where the closer the couple moves toward God, the closer they inevitably draw toward each other. It's amazing how clear things become when your compass isn't set on personal happiness alone, but on divine purpose.

Let's be honest, trying to do marriage solely on human strength is like trying to build furniture in a box without the instruction manual. You may get there eventually, but you'll cry at least once, and probably end up with leftover screws (or scars). Centering your relationship on God doesn't eliminate problems, but it radically shifts how you approach them: with grace instead of grudge, prayer instead of panic, and purpose instead of pettiness.

So as we jump into this next chapter, don't just think of it as a spiritual interlude, but as the sturdy foundation beneath all the love, laughs, and laundry piles. After all, when God isn't just an occasional guest in your marriage but the grounding presence at its core, you'll not only survive the tougher seasons, you'll actually grow stronger through them. Ready? Let's center up!

SPIRITUAL DISCIPLINES AS A COUPLE (PRAYER, BIBLE, WOR-SHIP)

A Christ-centered marriage doesn't happen by accident. It's not the result of just falling in love with someone who goes to church or shares your values. It's the fruit of consistent, intentional spiritual practices, what we often call spiritual disciplines. Just like athletes must train to perform at their peak, a couple must nurture certain habits if they want their relationship to reflect the heart of Christ. Without these disciplines, marriage can easily drift into autopilot, guided more by emotion or convenience than by faith.

At the core of these disciplines are prayer, Bible reading, and worship. Think of prayer as the lifeline of communication, not just between you and God, but also between each other. Praying together regularly keeps your hearts connected, not only spiritually, but emotionally. It's hard to stay bitter with someone you've just asked God to bless. Prayer builds unity, fosters humility, and invites the Holy Spirit to guide your conversations and your conflicts.

Then there's the Bible, your marriage's ultimate instruction manual. While marriage advice books and counselors' counsel can be invaluable, the Word of God remains the purest and most powerful source of wisdom. Reading scripture together reminds you of God's design for love, forgiveness, sacrifice, and grace. It keeps you rooted in truth, especially when your feelings might try to rewrite the story. Couples who choose to explore the Bible together discover a new depth of intimacy; they begin to speak the same spiritual language.

And let's not forget worship, not just the Sunday morning kind with music and coffee, but a lifestyle of placing God above all else in your home. When you worship together, you're realigning your hearts under God's authority. Whether that means singing together, sharing gratitude over dinner, or simply acknowledging God's goodness in everyday life, worship reminds both of you that your marriage isn't about making each other happy, it's about glorifying God. Happiness often follows, but His glory comes first.

Spiritual disciplines create the rhythm and structure that nurture a Christ-centered marriage. They don't guarantee perfection, but they do guarantee direction. When you're praying, engaging the Word, and worshiping together, you are intentionally inviting God into every room of your marriage, not just the Sunday-morning version, but the messy, beautiful, everyday walk. That's where true strength and unity are forged.

PRAYER IN MARRIAGE

Marriage sometimes feels like a three-legged race at a church picnic, you're tied together, you're trying to move forward, and if you're not in sync, someone's going face-first into the potato salad! That's why prayer isn't just a nice spiritual activity for married couples; it's essential. It's the powerful glue that invites God into the mess and helps align both spouses with His heart and with each other. Without prayer, you're doing marriage with a blindfold on, hoping your love alone will steer the ship. Spoiler alert: it won't!

The Bible makes it clear that prayer isn't just a suggestion; it's the lifeblood of a believer's relationship with God, and that includes in marriage. Jesus Himself says in Luke 18:1, *'They should always pray and not lose heart (give up).'* That's good advice for dealing with life's challenges, and even better advice for handling the silent treatment you might get after forgetting your anniversary. In marriage, prayer is like Wi-Fi; you might not see it, but when it's working, everything runs more smoothly. And when it's not? Well, suddenly nothing's connecting, and everyone's frustrated!

James 5:16 says, *'The prayer of a righteous person is powerful and effective.'* Imagine what that can do in a marriage when both spouses seek God together. It creates a spiritual unity that isn't built on moods or circumstances but on the eternal presence of God. Ecclesiastes 4:12 reminds us that a cord of three strands, husband, wife, and God, is not easily broken. That third strand doesn't appear on its own. It's braided in through intentional moments of shared prayer that welcome God into the center of everything: your hopes, decisions, frustrations, and dreams.

Picture two marriages side by side. One rarely prays, maybe says grace before dinner on a good day, but primarily operates out of human effort. They love each other, sure, but when conflict arises, they move to opposite emotional corners, ready for battle. The other makes prayer a daily rhythm, quiet moments of gratitude, whispered prayers before big decisions, and honest cries of 'Lord, help us' when the tension rises. The difference isn't in personalities or fewer arguments; it's in perspective, peace, and the Spirit's presence guiding their steps.

If you want a prayerful marriage, don't wait for a perfect schedule or a dramatic spiritual experience to kick it off. Start small. Maybe a few minutes before bed, holding hands and lifting up one another. Set an alarm in the morning to say a few words together before the day kicks your door in. Even if it feels awkward at first or one of you starts snoring in the middle, keep showing up. Because over time, prayer moves your marriage from surviving mode to thriving mode. It takes your conversations from surface-level to spirit-deep, and your connection from fragile to fortified. So, pray as your marriage depends on it, because it pretty much does.

BIBLE IN MARRIAGE

Staying rooted in the Bible is one of the most crucial elements for building and sustaining a God-centered marriage. The Bible isn't just a source of inspiration for tough days or a collection of poetic love verses for anniversaries; it is the unchanging truth that shapes how we love, serve, forgive, and grow in marriage. Without it, we're prone to drifting into cultural expectations, self-centered mindsets, or emotion-driven decisions. With it, we have a true north to guide us through every stage of the journey.

Psalm 119:105 reminds us, '*Your word is a lamp to my feet and a light to my path.*' In marriage, that light is essential for navigating the dim corridors of conflict, communication breakdowns, and even just figuring out who's responsible for the dishes. God's Word illuminates the way forward when our own understanding falls short. Ephesians 5, often called the marriage chapter, gives clear direction on sacrificial love, mutual respect, and spiritual leadership, not merely as sound advice, but as divine instruction. And 2 Timothy 3:16-17 tells us that all Scripture is God-breathed and useful for teaching, rebuking, correcting, and training in righteousness, which is precisely what every marriage needs regularly.

Now, contrast two marriages: in one, the couple rarely opens the Bible. Their values are shaped more by social media algorithms and personal preferences than by the Word of God. When disagreements arise, there's no higher authority to appeal to, just who can argue better, or who gives in first. Over time, emotions set the tone, and the relationship becomes reactive and unstable. In the other marriage, the couple regularly engages Scripture together. They don't just read it — they seek to live it. During disagreements, they can return not just to each other but to the truth of God's Word. Forgiveness flows more freely because they remember how much they themselves have been forgiven (Colossians 3:13). Selfishness gets challenged because they're reminded to consider others above themselves (Philippians 2:3-4).

Being rooted in the Bible doesn't mean you'll have a conflict-free, Pinterest-perfect marriage. What it does mean is that your marriage will be built on solid ground (Matthew 7:24-25). When the winds of stress, disappointment, or difficulty blow, and they will, your relationship won't collapse, because it's anchored in the timeless truth of God. Scripture gives you shared values, shared direction, and a shared foundation that lasts far longer than feelings. So don't just sprinkle a verse over your wedding vows and call it good. Let the Word of God saturate your home, your hearts, and your habits, because a Bible-rooted marriage is a strong, Christ-centered marriage.

WORSHIP IN MARRIAGE

Worship is one of the most overlooked, yet most potent weapons in a Christ-centered marriage. It's not just something we do on Sunday mornings when the worship team plays our favorite song; it's a lifestyle, a posture of the heart that keeps Christ enthroned in our relationship. Worship in marriage is how we actively fight back against the subtle and not-so-subtle attacks of the enemy. It shifts our focus from self to Savior, from tension to truth, and from fear to faith. Without it, we're trying to wage spiritual war with empty holsters.

Scripture makes it clear that worship is spiritual warfare. In 2 Chronicles 20:22, when enemy armies surrounded Judah, it wasn't swords and shields that won the battle — it was worship. The people began to sing and praise, and God confused their enemies and brought victory. Imagine bringing that same powerful principle into your marriage. Satan hates worship because he knows it disarms him and magnifies God's presence. As Ephesians 6:12 reminds us, 'For we do not *wrestle against flesh and blood, but against... spiritual forces of evil in the heavenly places.*' Worship is one of our most effective daily defenses.

But worship in a marriage goes beyond singing together, though that's a beautiful way to connect. Worship is every intentional act of placing God above ourselves. It's seen in choosing to forgive when it's hard (Colossians 3:13), in expressing gratitude to God together even during trials (1 Thessalonians 5:18), and in putting your spouse's needs before your own as an act of obedience (Philippians 2:3-4). Worship is lived out when a couple prays together before making a decision, chooses to go to church rather than sleep in, or speaks words of life over each other rather than criticism. It's not music that moves the enemy

39

away from your marriage; it's a life surrendered in reverence to Christ.

Compare a marriage that practices worship regularly to one that doesn't. In a marriage without worship, it's easy for stress, pride, and resentment to take the driver's seat. Everything becomes about winning arguments, protecting self-interest, or just surviving the chaos of life. The enemy thrives in that kind of environment, one where God is an afterthought. But in a worshipful marriage, God's presence is constantly invited in. Conflict becomes opportunities to grow, not just to fight. Joy is found beyond circumstances. The marriage becomes not just about two people trying to make it work, but about glorifying God through their love and unity.

In short, worship brings heaven's perspective into the center of earthly problems. It reminds us who God is, who we are, and where the real battle lies. When worship is central, the marriage becomes a fortress of praise that the enemy can't easily invade. So turn the key, open the door, and let true worship fill your marriage, not just on Sunday, but every single day.

GUARDING AGAINST IDOLATRY OF CAREER, KIDS, OR COMFORT

One of the quietest threats to a Christ-centered marriage isn't always blatant sin or conflict; it's misplaced priorities. Idolatry in marriage often sneaks in the back door, disguised as good things: a successful career, caring for the kids, or striving for a comfortable life. While these things aren't bad in and of themselves, they were never meant to take the top seats in your heart. In God's divine order for relationships, He should always be first, your spouse second, and everything else comes after that. When that order gets flipped, even unintentionally, the foundation of your marriage begins to crack.

Jesus makes the priority clear in Matthew 22:37-39 when He says the greatest commandment is to love the Lord your God with all your heart, soul, and mind, and then to love your neighbor as yourself. Your spouse, being your closest neighbor, comes right after your devotion to God. That means you don't serve your job, your kids, or your lifestyle above your marriage; they are gifts to be stewarded, not gods to be worshiped. Matthew 6:33 echoes this by reminding us to seek first the kingdom of God and His righteousness, and then all these things (including the provision for our families and careers) will be added to us.

Take, for example, a couple named Mark and Lisa. Mark was a dedicated professional, climbing the corporate ladder and often working late to secure a better life for his family. Lisa poured herself entirely into their children, every game, every play date, every need fulfilled. At first glance, they looked like a strong team. But years down the road, their marriage felt like two coworkers managing schedules rather than a deeply connected couple. They rarely spent time alone, stopped praying together, and God became a distant memory in their home life. When the kids grew up and their careers plateaued, they realized they had built their lives around things that couldn't sustain their relationship. With no spiritual foundation and little emotional connection left, they struggled to rediscover what once held them together.

Contrast that with a couple who intentionally put God first, starting each day in prayer, making worship part of their lifestyle, and setting aside time for one another, no matter how hectic life gets. They don't ignore their children or careers, but those things flow from a healthy, Christ-centered union. They navigate parenting as a united front and view work as a calling rather than an idol. Even in the toughest seasons, their marriage remains anchored because they haven't forgotten the order: God first, marriage second, and everything else finds its place behind that.

Idolatry may be subtle, but its effects are significant. When we elevate anything above God or above our marriage covenant, disconnection and dysfunction follow. But when we honor God by putting Him first and keeping our marriage close behind, we create a fertile ground for love, trust, joy, and lasting unity, not just in our relationship, but throughout our home.

THE MARRIAGE ALTAR: DAILY SURRENDER

The real marriage altar isn't just the rose-petaled platform you stood on the day you said your vows; it's the place you return to every single day in your heart. A Christ-centered marriage is built not just on one big 'I do,' but on many small, daily surrenders. It's waking up every morning and deciding again to lay down selfish desires, to forgive offenses, to serve instead of demand, and to love the way Christ loves us. It's this continuous posture of surrender that keeps the altar burning and Christ at the center.

Romans 12:1 says, '*Therefore, I urge you, brothers and sisters, in view of God's mercy, to offer your bodies as a living sacrifice, holy and pleasing to God—this is your true and proper worship.*' That isn't just an individual challenge; it applies to every couple seriously aiming for a God-centered marriage. The idea here isn't a one-and-done sacrifice, but a living sacrifice, ongoing, active, deliberate. Your marriage becomes an altar where two people continuously offer themselves to God, laying down pride, fear, insecurity, and agenda.

Philippians 2:5-8 reminds us to have the same attitude as Christ, who humbled Himself and became obedient, even to death on a cross. Marriage demands that same humility, not to die physically (though some arguments might come close!), but to die daily to the me-first mindset that the world promotes. A Christ-centered marriage will thrive when both husband and wife are more interested in reflecting Jesus than in winning the latest disagreement. That kind of posture doesn't just preserve a marriage — it transforms it.

So as we wrap up this chapter, remember this: a marriage with God at the center isn't built by accident or based on feelings; it's lived out in daily decisions. Decisions to pray together, to stay rooted in God's Word, to worship in the everyday, and to guard your relationship from idolatry. And most importantly, to keep coming back to the altar of surrender. When couples lay themselves down in humility before Christ, He lifts their marriage up in strength, grace, and purpose.

You don't need a perfect marriage; you need a surrendered one. Because when you both submit your hearts to Jesus, He can take your ordinary love story and turn it into something extraordinary for His glory.

Marriage as a Mission – Reflection & Action Guide
Reflection Questions

1. What competes most for Christ's place at the center of your marriage?
2. How consistent are you in spiritual practices together (prayer, worship, Scripture)?

43

3. When have you felt most spiritually connected as a couple?

Mission in Action

- Set aside 10 minutes daily this week to pray together.
- Choose one Bible passage to read and discuss as a couple (e.g., Psalm 1 or Colossians 3).
- Identify one idol (career, kids, comfort) and talk about how to re-center Christ.

5. Roles with a Purpose

I f you've ever put together a piece of furniture without the instructions, only to end up sitting on what looks more like a modern art sculpture than a coffee table, then you already understand the importance of design. Marriage is no different. Except instead of leftover screws, you wind up with unresolved arguments and bewildered expressions. But here's the good news: God hasn't left us to figure it all out with an Allen wrench and hope. He has a design for our marriages, and each role in that relationship actually serves a greater purpose.

It's easy in the chaos of everyday life to forget that marriage wasn't just humanity's idea; it was God's. From the very beginning, He created it with intention and detail. That means your marriage isn't some random cosmic event, but a piece of a divine masterpiece. It's a bit like a duet: two different instruments intended to play in harmony, not in unison. When each plays their part, the result is beautiful. When they try to outdo each other? Well, let's say the audience might run for cover!

Now, this divine design isn't about one being better, louder, or more in control than the other. It's about roles that complement each other, like peanut butter and jelly, or coffee and cream. Each one brings something essential to the table, and without both, something gets lost. The balance doesn't mean everything is always fifty-fifty; it means that when each person lives out their role with purpose, the whole marriage works better. Even if sometimes it feels like one of you is from Mars and the other is just trying to find the remote.

Of course, understanding that there is a God-given design in marriage doesn't mean figuring it out is always easy. In fact, sometimes it feels like trying to assemble that metaphorical furniture with instructions written in another language. But here's the key: it's not about perfection — it's about intentionality. Recognizing that God has placed purpose in your role, and that role exists not just for your benefit, but for the strength of your marriage and the reflection of His love through it.

So before we get into the specifics of who does what and why, take heart. You're not stumbling through your marriage blindly or randomly. God has written the blueprints. And when we begin to follow His design, on purpose and with purpose, something extraordinary can happen right in the middle of ordinary daily life. So get ready, this chapter is where the pieces start to come together.

GOD'S DESIGN FOR HUSBANDS AND WIVES

When it comes to defining the roles of husbands and wives, the Bible is not vague or abstract; it's actually quite clear and straightforward. God, in His infinite wisdom, designed marriage as a partnership in which both husband and wife are equal in value yet distinct in function. Think of it this way: a football team doesn't work if everyone insists on being the quarterback. Someone has to snap the ball, someone has to block, and yes, someone has to yell audibles (that's usually the husband). In the same way, God assigns key roles to both partners in marriage, not to create an imbalance but to foster harmony that reflects His own nature and purpose.

Let's start with the husband. According to Ephesians 5:23, '*For the husband is the head of the wife even as Christ is the head of the church, his body, and is himself its Savior.*' That's a weighty job. Being the 'head' doesn't mean being the dictator of the house, bossing everyone around with a TV remote scepter. Instead, it's a call to loving leadership, much like Christ leads the Church, with sacrifice, humility, and grace. Verse 25 of that same chapter lays it out clearly: '*Husbands, love your wives, as Christ loved the church and gave himself up for her.*' If that sounds like a high bar, it's because it is. Leadership in God's design is about service, not superiority.

Now wives, before you roll your eyes and mutter something about patriarchy under your breath, let's take a look at your role (which, by the way, is equally valuable and seriously powerful). Ephesians 5:22 says, '*Wives, submit to your own husbands, as to the Lord.*' This is not a command to follow someone blindly or to be seen and not heard. Biblical submission is willingly coming under the loving leadership of your husband, not because you're a lesser person, but because you're choosing to trust in God's design. It's like partnering in a dance, only one person leads, but both have to move in sync, or someone's toes get stepped on. And for the record, biblical submission is never about silent suffering or accepting abuse; it's about mutual love and respect under God's authority.

It's also important to clarify that, although God gives husbands a position of authority, it is not a license to control or dominate. Galatians 3:28 reminds us, '*There is neither Jew nor Greek, there is neither slave nor free, there is no male and female,*

47

for you are all one in Christ Jesus.' This shows that when it comes to our value before God, there is complete and total equality. Husbands and wives are co-heirs of grace (1 Peter 3:7), fellow image-bearers, and both are held accountable to God. The biblical model of marriage is not a boss-employee structure; it's more like a CEO and COO running the same company with different responsibilities, but equal shares in the mission.

Let's also not forget the practical outcomes of these roles. When the husband leads with love and the wife respects that leadership, it sets the tone for a home where peace can flourish, kids can thrive, and everyone can find safety and purpose. Colossians 3:18-19 echoes the roles again: *'Wives, submit to your husbands, as is fitting in the Lord. Husbands, love your wives, and do not be harsh with them.'* Scripture gives us this structure not to limit either spouse, but to free them to be who they were designed to be, together.

In the end, marriage isn't about one person getting their way. It's about both people walking in their God-given roles, reflecting something much bigger, the relationship between Christ and His Church. God's design is precise and intentional, not outdated or oppressive. So whether you're the one who fixes the leaking faucet or the one who knows how to fix everyone's emotional crisis, your role matters. And when both husband and wife embrace those roles with humility and humor (because trust me, you're going to need both), they'll discover that God's blueprint for marriage is not only purposeful — it's beautiful. Even if sometimes it takes a little trial and a lot of grace to get all the parts in place.

It's no surprise that Satan despises the biblical design of marriage. From the very beginning, he has sought to distort, divide, and destroy anything that reflects God's image, and marriage does precisely that. God's design for husband and wife to become one flesh (Genesis 2:24) is a sacred reflection of Christ's relationship with the Church (Ephesians 5:31-32). That alone makes marriage a top target on the enemy's hit list. Satan doesn't just want to give your family a bad day; he wants to unravel God's entire blueprint for the home because it represents covenant, unity, and godly purpose.

Just look at how early on in Scripture we see the enemy launch his attack on the first marriage. In Genesis 3, Satan approached Eve in the garden, not only seeking to lead her into sin but to disrupt the divine order God had established. Adam and Eve's unity was broken, shame entered, and blame followed. The family, as it was designed, fell into disarray, and that pattern hasn't stopped. Satan knows that if he can destroy the family, he can disrupt generations. He attacks communication between spouses, sows seeds of bitterness, tempts with selfishness, and pushes culture to distort gender roles and redefine marriage altogether.

Why does he do this? Because the family, at its core, is the front line of spiritual formation. Deuteronomy 6:6-7 tells us to teach God's commands diligently to our children, to speak of them at home, throughout the day, making faith a natural part of family life. Strong marriages breed strong families, and strong families build strong communities and churches. That's a direct threat to the kingdom of darkness. No wonder he unleashes his tactics with such fury and subtlety.

But here's the good news: Satan may hate biblical marriage, but he doesn't have the final word. Through Jesus Christ, we are given everything we need to overcome the enemy's schemes. James 4:7 says, '*Submit yourselves therefore to God. Resist the devil, and he will flee from you.*' A marriage rooted in Christ is

49

not only protected; it's powerful. 2 Corinthians 10:4-5 reminds us that '*the weapons of our warfare are not of the flesh but have divine power to destroy strongholds.*' In Christ, we have authority over every attempt of the enemy to steal peace, joy, or unity from our homes.

So yes, Satan rages against godly families and the roles each spouse holds. He mocks purity, opposes submission, twists authority, and delights in division. But a marriage built on the foundation of Jesus is not easily shaken. As Romans 8:37 reminds us, '*No, in all these things we are more than conquerors through him who loved us.*' The victory doesn't come from trying harder but from surrendering to Jesus and trusting that His design, though often challenged, is good, perfect, and ultimately triumphant. Even on the hard days, God's grace is enough to hold your family firm in a fallen world.

SERVANT LEADERSHIP VS. CULTURAL DISTORTIONS OF AUTHORITY

God's design for leadership in marriage is all about servant-heartedness, not domination. When He gives roles and authority within marriage, especially to husbands as the spiritual leaders of the home, it's never about power plays or self-serving control. Instead, it mirrors the way Jesus leads His Church, with compassion, humility, love, and sacrifice. In fact, Jesus Himself redefined leadership when He said in Matthew 20:26-28, '*Whoever would be great among you must be your servant...even as the Son of Man came not to be served but to serve, and to give his life as a ransom for many.*' That's the model God wants husbands to follow: leadership that bends low for the good of the other.

Unfortunately, culture often gets this completely backward.

The moment you mention words like authority or headship, alarms go off and accusations start flying. That's because society tends to associate authority with dominance or abuse, thanks to far too many misuses of leadership in and outside the home. As a result, the biblical idea of a husband's leadership is often either ridiculed or completely rejected. But God's version of leadership defies worldly expectations; it's not about control, it's about commitment. It's not about being the boss; it's about bearing the weight of responsibility for the family with gentleness and integrity.

Ephesians 5:25 isn't a power trip; it's a call to selflessness: '*Husbands, love your wives, as Christ loved the church and gave himself up for her.*' That kind of love doesn't bark orders or lay down ultimatums. It washes feet, listens patiently, and sacrifices even when it goes unnoticed. And wives, your biblical response to that kind of leadership, according to Ephesians 5:22-24, is one of trust and support. It's not about being less than; it's about walking in unity and honoring the mission God has given you together.

When culture distorts this picture, marriages suffer. Authority becomes confused with entitlement. Submission becomes equated with weakness. Nobody wants to be led, and few want to lead with humility. But when we understand God's design for servant leadership, it flips the script. There is great strength in leading like Jesus, and deep beauty in coming alongside and supporting that leadership. Both husband and wife have equal value and dignity; their roles are simply different by divine design.

In the end, servant leadership in marriage reflects the heart of the gospel. It's putting the other person first. It's taking responsibility, not for personal gain, but for the good of the home. Just like Jesus didn't lord over the disciples but knelt to serve them, God calls husbands to lead with that same posture. That's not outdated or oppressive, it's revolutionary, and it's precisely what our homes and our broken world desperately need.

A great example of servant leadership in marriage is when a husband takes the initiative to serve his wife, not because he has to, but because he wants to reflect Christ's love. Imagine this: after a long day at work, the husband comes home and finds his wife overwhelmed with the kids, the laundry piling up, and dinner still a question mark. Instead of collapsing on the couch and disappearing into the sports channel abyss, he steps in. He helps with the dinner, folds some clothes, and wrangles the kids for bedtime. Not because he's trying to earn points, but because he values his wife and sees loving her well as a leadership responsibility.

Now, in God's design, that is beautiful. It's a picture of mutual love and selflessness that strengthens the marriage. But culture might look at that same situation and say something like, 'Wow, he's whipped,' or 'He must be under her thumb.' The act of humble sacrifice, rather than being admired, is often mocked as a sign of weakness. On the flip side, if a wife willingly respects and supports her husband's leadership in the home, culture might perceive it as being old-fashioned, oppressed, or lacking independence.

The distortion lies in how culture sees power. The world often preaches that leadership is about control and dominance. So when someone leads by serving, or when someone supports another's leadership, it doesn't fit the cultural narrative of self-promotion and personal gain. That's why servant leadership looks upside-down to many, because it really is. Jesus flipped the leadership model on its head, showing us that the greatest among us is the one who serves (Matthew 23:11). But to a culture that values assertiveness over humility, that kind of leadership can seem weak and even foolish.

What God calls strength, the world sometimes calls weakness. But within a biblical marriage, servant leadership is one of the most powerful ways to demonstrate God's love in action. It requires courage, humility, and a heart anchored in something far deeper than ego or cultural trends. And while the world may misinterpret it, a home where servant leadership thrives is full of peace, respect, and the kind of joy that isn't easily shaken.

UNITY AND COMPLEMENTARITY IN ACTION

Unity and complementarity in a biblical marriage are like two hands working together, different in structure but created to perform the same task in harmony. It's not about one person doing everything or being in charge of everything; it's about each spouse embracing their God-given role to build a unified, Christ-centered team. When both husband and wife understand and live out their distinct roles, the result is not competition, but cooperation. And that unity is a powerful witness to the world of what godly love really looks like.

For example, imagine a season in which a husband is working full-time, and the wife is staying home with young children. The husband provides for the family financially while the wife nurtures the home and helps shape the kids' spiritual and emotional growth. Each plays a different role, yet both work toward the same goal, providing for and caring for their household. If the husband tried to do it all while never supporting his wife, or if the wife refused to acknowledge his leadership and continually undermined him, the unity would begin to crack. But when they support each other's roles and see the value in one another's contributions, their marriage reflects the peace, order, and harmony that God designed.

Complementarity also shows up in how decisions are made. In a biblical marriage, while the husband is the head of the home (Ephesians 5:23), that doesn't mean he acts like a one-man board of directors. A wise husband values his wife's wisdom and perspective. Proverbs 31:11 says, *'The heart of her husband trusts in her, and he will have no lack of gain.'* That trust means decisions are discussed together with mutual respect, and the husband, in his role, considers her thoughts carefully before leading the family forward. Unity isn't found in one person always negotiating their desires away; it's found when both are pulling in the same direction, even when one is steering.

Another practical picture of complementarity is in spiritual growth. A husband leading the way in reading Scripture together, praying as a couple, or setting a Christlike tone in the home is servant leadership in action. The wife, in turn, can encourage and support him while also using her own spiritual gifts to edify the family, whether through discipleship of the kids, offering advice in difficult seasons, or speaking truth in love. They both play essential roles in shaping a Christ-centered home, and neither role is less than the other.

This unity and complementarity are not just for ease in managing daily tasks; they preach the gospel. Ephesians 5:31–32 reminds us that marriage is a mystery that points to Christ and the Church. Just as Christ leads with love and the Church responds with trust and devotion, husbands and wives reflect that divine relationship through their unity and distinct roles. When marriage works the way God intended, it's not only a blessing to the couple, it's a powerful display of God's truth and grace to a watching world. That's why embracing unity and complementarity matters: it glorifies God, strengthens the marriage, and leaves a legacy of faith for generations to come.

Marriage as a Mission – Reflection & Action Guide
Reflection Questions

1. How have cultural messages shaped your view of marital roles?
2. What does servant leadership look like for a husband?
3. How can wives practice respect in a way that honors both Christ and their husband?

Mission in Action

- Each of you write down what you most need from your spouse in their role. Share and discuss.
- Read Philippians 2:3-4 and talk about how humility can shape your roles.
- Pray for God to help you embrace His design, not the world's distortions.

6. Love that Serves and Forgives

Marriage, at its foundation, is not merely an agreement or partnership; it is a covenant shaped by love that both serves and forgives. In a world where relationships are often defined by personal gain and fleeting emotions, the covenant of marriage calls us into a deeper, selfless relationship. Love, as expressed within marriage, transcends feeling; it becomes a daily act of choosing the other person, even when it hurts, even when it costs something, and especially when it demands grace.

This chapter represents the heart of a thriving marriage. Serving in love means putting the well-being and needs of your spouse before your own, not out of obligation, but as a joyful response to the commitment you've made. Forgiveness, likewise, becomes the oil that keeps the relationship running smoothly, especially when wounds are inevitable. Neither service nor forgiveness is a weakness; they are the strength behind enduring love.

Such a love cannot be sustained merely by human effort. It is rooted in the divine example of Christ, who served sacrificially and forgave fully. His model gives couples a vision for what marriage can look like when it is not based on performance or perfection, but on grace and daily surrender. In this kind of love, failures do not end the relationship but become opportunities for growth, humility, and renewed closeness.

This chapter will explore what it really means to love one another with hearts eager to serve and ready to forgive. It will offer insight into how these twin pillars support not only the structure of marriage but also its beauty. As we journey forward, we will uncover the practical expressions of sacrificial love and the deep healing that forgiveness brings to a lifelong union.

PRACTICING UNCONDITIONAL LOVE AND FORGIVENESS

Unconditional love and forgiveness are not just good ideas for a biblical marriage — they're essential. Without them, marriage becomes a transactional relationship that can easily crumble under pressure. But with them, marriage becomes a reflection of God's covenant with His people: enduring, merciful, and full of grace. To understand this kind of love, we don't have to look far in the Bible. One of the most powerful examples comes from Hosea, yes, the prophet with the unorthodox love life.

God instructed Hosea to marry Gomer, a woman who would repeatedly betray him. Gomer's repeated unfaithfulness was meant to illustrate Israel's unfaithfulness to God, but it also highlights the staggering nature of unconditional love. Hosea loved Gomer not because of her performance or reliability, but because God called him to demonstrate a love that pursues despite betrayal. Now, no one is recommending you marry a person bent on unfaithfulness, but the principle here is key: real love, covenant love, doesn't quit when the warm feelings fade or hurt enters the picture.

Unconditional love in marriage looks like putting your spouse's needs ahead of your own, even when they are being exceptionally unlovable. It means speaking kindly when you're tired and they're cranky, choosing grace when they've forgotten something important, and staying faithful even when you're the only one trying for a season. Attaining this kind of love requires staying close to the source, God Himself. As 1 John 4:19 reminds us, '*We love because He first loved us.*' You can't sustain unconditional love on willpower alone. It comes from being regularly filled with God's love through prayer, the Word, and asking God daily to give you His heart for your spouse.

And then there's forgiveness, the daily bread of every good marriage. If unconditional love is the house of marriage, forgiveness is the plumbing. Without it, things start to build up, stagnate, and eventually cause a flood. A beautiful biblical picture of forgiveness can be seen in Joseph. Although not in a marriage context, his story holds a powerful example. After being betrayed by his own brothers, sold into slavery, and forgotten for years, Joseph finally had the power to get even. Instead, he chose mercy. He gave what they didn't deserve, echoing the very heart of what God does for us.

True forgiveness in marriage means letting go of the right to punish. It's not the same as pretending nothing happened or excusing hurtful behavior, but it is choosing not to hold the offense as a debt. It means when your spouse forgets an anniversary, speaks harshly, or wounds you deeply, you process the hurt but refuse to use it as a future weapon. Attaining this kind of forgiveness is humanly impossible without God. It takes prayer, time, and a continual reminder of how much you've been forgiven. Ephesians 4:32 says, '*Be kind and compassionate to one another, forgiving each other, just as in Christ God forgave you.*' Remembering God's mercy toward us fuels our ability to extend it.

Let's be honest, sometimes, the irritations of daily married life can make forgiveness feel extra challenging, like when your spouse leaves dishes in the sink 'to soak'... for three days. Or when the toothpaste tube is squeezed from the middle again. But true forgiveness learns not to let minor annoyances build into major grievances. It confronts in love when needed, but also learns to overlook. Proverbs 19:11 says, '*It is to one's glory to overlook an offense.*' In other words, it's not a weakness to let things go sometimes — it's wisdom.

Cultivating unconditional love and true forgiveness in marriage is a lifelong process. It won't happen without failure, but the grace of marriage is that you get to practice every day. As you learn to love deeply and forgive freely, your marriage becomes not just a union of two people, but a testimony of God's character displayed in a human relationship. And the good news? When God is the one holding your marriage together, He also supplies the strength you need to love without limits and forgive without keeping score.

Unforgiveness is one of the enemy's most effective tools for destroying a marriage, as it subtly poisons the relationship from within. Satan knows he doesn't need to launch massive attacks when he can simply plant seeds of bitterness and resentment that go unchecked. When a couple allows unresolved hurt to linger, it builds an emotional wall between them. Communication breaks down, intimacy wanes, and instead of feeling like teammates, spouses start viewing each other as opponents.

Scripture warns us clearly about this danger. In Ephesians 4:26-27, Paul writes, '*Do not let the sun go down while you are still angry, and do not give the devil a foothold.*' That word, foothold, is key. It suggests a position of access, an open door for Satan to exploit. When forgiveness is withheld, it's like handing the devil a key to the front door of your marriage. He uses that access to distort perspectives, escalate minor issues into major battles, and convince each spouse that the other is the enemy.

Over time, unforgiveness transforms minor offenses into deep wounds that rewrite how spouses see each other. A careless comment turns into proof of rejection. A forgotten promise becomes undeniable evidence of neglect. The enemy is a master at using these moments to sow division, isolation, and, eventually, hopelessness. Many marriages that end in emotional or legal separation don't do so because of one major betrayal, but because of years of small, unattended hurts that were never healed through forgiveness.

That's why forgiveness isn't optional in a healthy, godly marriage — it's central. It's the guardrail that keeps a couple's heart soft toward each other, even in conflict. Forgiveness keeps the channel of grace open, allowing healing and restoration to flow freely. It breaks the enemy's grip and reinforces unity. When spouses regularly confess fault, extend grace, and refuse to keep score, they fortify their marriage with a spiritual armor Satan cannot easily penetrate. Forgiveness doesn't mean pretending pain didn't happen; it means choosing love over revenge, healing over keeping score, and long-term unity over short-term self-righteousness.

A forgiving marriage is a resilient, spiritually protected one. By choosing to make forgiveness a central habit and fruit in the relationship, couples close the door on the enemy and create an atmosphere where love, peace, and God's presence can thrive.

BREAKING CYCLES OF BITTERNESS

Bitterness in marriage often begins with a single unresolved hurt. Maybe it's a cutting comment during an argument, a forgotten promise, or a pattern of neglect that goes unaddressed. At first, it might seem small, something we think we can shrug off. But when that hurt is not spoken about or healed through honest communication and forgiveness, it settles into the heart. Over time, it becomes a filter through which everything in the marriage is seen. What was once a simple offense grows into growing discontent, and before long, every word or action by the spouse is interpreted through that unresolved wound.

That initial wound, left unchecked, can easily lead to resentment. Resentment is the poisonous root of bitterness, an inner posture that keeps a mental account of wrongs. This could sound like, 'He always lets me down,' or 'She never appreciates what I do.' The deeper this root grows, the more it affects a spouse's thoughts, tone, and even body language. Once resentment has taken hold, it affects how one reacts in conflicts, how they speak to each other, and whether they show affection. The home grows colder, and tension mounts, and compassion begins to fade.

Bitterness often functions in a damaging cycle. One spouse feels offended or overlooked, which leads to silent frustration. That silence becomes emotional distance, and the other spouse picks up on it, feeling hurt by the withdrawal and responding with their own form of defensiveness or passivity. Now both people feel wounded and misunderstood, but no one is addressing the core issue. Over time, apologies become scarce, assumptions take over, and the couple starts building walls rather than bridges. The longer bitterness remains unhealed, the harder it is to remember why they were drawn to each other in the first place.

What makes this cycle even more dangerous is that bitterness doesn't stay quiet forever. Eventually, it comes out, usually during moments of high stress or conflict. Old wounds are suddenly brought up in present conversations, and arguments become overloaded with past offenses rather than present concerns. The couple isn't fighting about what happened five minutes ago; they're fighting about what happened five months or five years ago. This is why Ephesians 4:31 warns us to '*get rid of all bitterness, rage and anger,*' because these emotions left unchecked will rot the foundation of a loving, unified marriage.

Breaking the cycle of bitterness requires intentional effort from both spouses, starting with humility and communication. It means being willing to honestly admit hurt feelings, forgiving as Christ forgave, and refusing to carry silent grievances that fester into deeper problems. It also means practicing grace, recognizing that our spouse is imperfect and will fall short at times, just like we do. Forgiveness isn't about forgetting what happened, but about choosing to let go of the offense and choosing peace over punishment.

If bitterness has already taken root, healing won't happen overnight. Still, when a couple decides to confront it together, with God's help, prayer, and maybe even wise counsel, the cycle can be broken. Love can be restored, trust can be rebuilt, and joy can return. A marriage free of bitterness isn't a perfect marriage, but it is one where grace flows freely, and where both spouses are committed to healing rather than hurting each other. That kind of marriage stands firm, even through storms.

James and Natalie had been married for twelve years when their relationship began to unravel. Things had started out well; they were active in their church, loved spending time together, and had two beautiful children. But over time, life brought the usual pressures: work stress, parenting challenges, and financial strain. Communication began to suffer. Natalie felt unsupported and unappreciated in her role at home, while James felt criticized and disrespected. Rather than addressing offenses with grace, they each began silently accumulating resentment.

What began as minor frustrations quickly grew into deep-rooted bitterness. James withdrew emotionally, seeking comfort in long hours at work, while Natalie stewed in loneliness and did her best to hold things together. Arguments became more frequent, but they weren't about the real issues; they were surface-level fights with years of unspoken pain underneath. At one point, they stopped praying together and rarely spoke without tension. Their hearts were wounded, and both believed they had fallen out of love. It seemed like divorce was the only way out of the cold war that had developed in their home.

But God wasn't finished with their story. Natalie, in desperation, poured out her heart to God and sought counsel from a wise, older couple at church. She began to ask God to help her forgive, not just in words, but from the heart. She realized that the bitterness in her life had not only impacted her marriage but also her relationship with God. James, separately, had a similar awakening after attending a men's retreat. Hearing testimonies of broken marriages restored brought him to tears, and he was moved to repentance over his pride and emotional distance.

The two began a long, honest journey back to healing. It started with a single, humble conversation where both admitted their pain, their faults, and their desire to try again, with Christ at the center. They began praying together again, started seeing a Christian counselor, and most importantly, embraced the habit of quick forgiveness and open communication. Slowly, the walls came down. Love didn't magically fix everything overnight, but day by day, as they chose humility, grace, and patience, trust was rebuilt. The bitterness that once ruled their home was replaced with peace.

The application is simple but powerful: don't underestimate what God can restore when two people humble themselves before Him. A bitter marriage isn't a hopeless marriage, unless both people stop fighting for it. If resentment has crept into your relationship, ask God to help you see your spouse through His eyes. Choose to forgive, not because they always deserve it, but because you've been forgiven so much yourself. Replace silence with honest, gracious conversations. Seek God together. Just like James and Natalie, restoration is possible, not because of human strength, but because nothing is impossible with God.

MARRIAGE AS A SCHOOL OF GRACE

Marriage is more than just a partnership; it's one of God's most hands-on classrooms for learning grace. In fact, few places require more consistent grace than life with another imperfect human being, especially one who tends to steal your side of the bed (and the sheets), forgets to take out the trash, or somehow can't hear the baby crying in the middle of the night. But really, in the very heart of daily frustrations and shared responsibilities, God uses marriage to teach us what it truly means to love like Him, through grace that is unearned, undeserved, and often uncomfortable.

In Titus 2:11, Paul tells us that '*For the grace of God has appeared, bringing salvation for all people.*' What's beautiful is that grace doesn't just save us, it trains us. And nowhere is that training ground more present than marriage. Think of marriage as a 'grace boot camp.' It's where we learn to extend kindness when we're hurt, patience when we're irritated, and forgiveness when we'd rather sulk. It's where we learn, daily, that love is not based on performance but on choice, a choice to keep showing up with compassion and mercy, just as God continually does for us.

Ephesians 4:2-3 echoes this very call: '*Be completely humble and gentle; be patient, bearing with one another in love. Make every effort to keep the unity of the Spirit through the bond of peace.*' The phrase 'bearing with one another' is not just poetic — it's realistic. Some days in marriage, bearing with one another looks like laughing instead of lashing out, choosing calm when fatigue says otherwise, or forgiving the toothbrush left in the sink again. Grace in marriage happens not just through grand gestures, but in simple, daily decisions to give more than we think we have.

But God doesn't ask us to give grace in marriage without showing us how. In fact, our relationships are intended to mirror the grace-filled relationship Christ has with the Church. Ephesians 5:25 says, '*Husbands, love your wives, just as Christ loved the church and gave himself up for her.*' That sets the bar pretty high. Jesus didn't love the Church when she was tidy and well-behaved. He loved relentlessly, washed feet, bore with flaws, and ultimately gave His life. That's the kind of grace that transforms hearts, and the kind we're invited to live out each day in marriage.

The beauty of it all is that when we show grace to our spouse, undeserved kindness, patience, and love, we're giving the world a glimpse of God. We're displaying what it looks like to experience mercy over merit, love over judgment, and unity over pride. Marriage, then, becomes a living parable of God's covenant with us. And yes, we'll mess it up. There will be days when grace feels far away, and irritation feels far too comfortable. But God isn't grading us on perfection; He's forming us through the process.

So if you've burned the toast, miscommunicated (again), or snapped because the toilet seat was left up for the thousandth time, take heart. These moments are not just obstacles; they're opportunities. Opportunities to learn what God's grace looks like in action, to show love without conditions, and to let God refine us through the most unexpected classroom: our own marriage. After all, what better place to learn grace than with the person you promised to walk with through it all, even when their sock ends up in the refrigerator (yes, that happens).

Marriage as a Mission – Reflection & Action Guide
  Reflection Questions

1. What small acts of service mean the most to you?
2. How do you typically handle offense? Do you withdraw, retaliate, or forgive quickly?
3. Where do you need to extend forgiveness right now?

Mission in Action

- Perform one act of service for your spouse daily this week without being asked.
- Share one area where you need forgiveness, then extend grace to one another.
- Pray the Lord's Prayer together, focusing on "forgive us as we forgive."

Part 3: Mission In Everyday Life

7. Marriage and Parenting as Discipleship

I t all started at 2:47 a.m. on a Wednesday — a time when nothing good ever happens unless you're a raccoon or an owl. My wife, Michelle, and I were deep in our REM cycles when a tiny voice whispered three feet from my face, 'I'm scared.' I opened my eyes to two bright white eyes staring at me in the dark at eye level. I just about had a heart attack!

There's no manual for that. Marriage didn't prepare me for it. All those once-romantic late-night talks we had before kids are now replaced with bleary-eyed negotiations about who's going to handle the potty disaster. It's always a debate, and somehow, every argument includes a detailed breakdown of who cleaned what bodily fluid last time.

Parenting in marriage is a beautiful chaos. One moment you're arguing over who left the milk out, and the next, you're tackling a trigonometry of lunchbox packing, favorite spoons, and whose turn it is to explain to a kindergartner why we don't yell 'I farted' in public.

And when you think you've got it figured out, like you remembered the field trip form and successfully fed everyone real vegetables, your toddler shaves the dog. With your razor. The same one you didn't know they could reach!

It's teamwork, yes. But it's also a survival sport. Marriage as parents feels less like a rom-com and more like a buddy cop film, where both leads are under-caffeinated, covered in applesauce, and trying to keep the baby from writing all over the walls with a crayon!

So here's to parenting in marriage, where the love is deep, the sleep is shallow, and every day brings a plot twist even Netflix couldn't write!

God entrusted us with the mission of parenting as part of His design for families, and Scripture offers guidance to support this sacred calling. From the very beginning, God entrusted humanity with the responsibility of raising and nurturing children.

In Genesis 1:28, God blessed Adam and Eve and said, '*Be fruitful and multiply, and fill the earth and subdue it.*' This wasn't just about population growth; it was a divine calling to raise up future generations who would walk in a relationship with Him. Parenting was God's idea from the start, and it's a partnership with Him in shaping human souls.

Proverbs 22:6 reinforces the intentional role we're given: '*Train up a child in the way he should go, and when he is old he will not depart from it.*' As parents, we're not just making school lunches and cleaning up LEGOs; we're actively guiding and shaping a child's life, helping them build a foundation that will carry them into adulthood.

Deuteronomy 6:6-7 further emphasizes our responsibility: '*And these words that I command you today shall be on your heart. You shall teach them diligently to your children, and shall talk of them when you sit in your house, and when you walk by the way, and when you lie down, and when you rise.*' God clearly designed parenting as a daily, life-integrated mission. It's not a part-time role — it's a full-life calling.

Psalm 127:3-4 reminds us of the blessing and purpose that children bring: '*Behold, children are a heritage from the Lord, the fruit of the womb a reward. Like arrows in the hand of a warrior are the children of one's youth.*' We're not just raising kids; we're launching future leaders, worshipers, and world-changers.

In short, parenting is not just a practical job — it's a divine assignment. God entrusts us with the care, guidance, and spiritual formation of the next generation. It's hard, yes, but it's holy.

MODELING CHRIST FOR CHILDREN

As parents, whether we realize it or not, we are walking billboards for how Christ loves the Church, and kids have front-row seats. Before they can even spell 'grace,' they are watching us live it out (or... not) in the everyday, often chaotic, jungle of home life. Our marriage becomes their first lens for understanding concepts like love, sacrifice, forgiveness, humility, and even conflict resolution, and that lens is powerful.

According to Ephesians 5:25, Paul writes, '*Husbands, love your wives, just as Christ loved the church and gave himself up for her.*' That's not just marriage advice; it's a parenting lesson, too, because our kids are watching how we love each other. Every moment we choose patience over sarcasm, forgiveness over pettiness, and kindness over grumbling, we're giving our kids a real, breathing example of Christlike love in action.

In that same chapter, Ephesians 5:22-23 speaks about mutual respect and structure within the marriage. Now, this part may elicit some controversy, depending on how you read it, but the chief takeaway for kids is not about hierarchical roles.

Christian marriage is indeed built on mutual sacrifice, unity, and honoring God. When kids see parents navigating challenges together with grace, they begin to connect the dots: 'Oh... this is what faith looks like in real life. Not just Sunday morning. But Thursday night in traffic. Or during the bedtime standoff over brushing teeth.'

And let's be honest: kids don't learn kindness when everyone's well-rested and the Wi-Fi is working. They learn it when your toddler is trying to flush your phone, your spouse just accidentally burned the dinner (again), and you both manage to laugh instead of having a meltdown. That's when Christ is most tangibly modeled.

Deuteronomy 6:6-7 reminds us that God's commands should be on our hearts and taught diligently to our children, whether we are sitting, walking, lying down, or rising. In other words, every moment is teachable. It's not about hosting a weekly devotional with puppets and snack platters (though if you do that, more power to you). It's about how we live, love, confess when we're wrong, and lean on God's grace in the everyday grind.

Now, here's the sobering news. Studies consistently show that when parents do not model a vibrant, Christ-centered faith, children are much less likely to carry faith into adulthood. According to data from the National Study of Youth and Religion (NSYR), one of the best predictors of a young adult's faith is the religious commitment of their parents. Specifically, the 2005 study found that teens who saw consistent, authentic faith practiced in their homes were significantly more likely to remain spiritually active. In fact, research published in the book 'Handing Down the Faith' (by Christian Smith and Amy Adamczyk, 2021) concludes that parents are by far the most influential factor in a child's spiritual development, far more than church, youth group, or their peers.

On the flip side, when Christ isn't genuinely modeled at home, kids often conclude that faith is just a mask we wear to church. And guess what? As soon as they're old enough to remove it, they do. Instagram won't tell them how to imitate Christ. TikTok sure won't. If they don't see Christ in us, they may not go looking for Him elsewhere.

So, as Christian parents, we don't just have a role, we have a mission. An audience. A discipleship program running daily in our living room that often smells like fish sticks and feet. We're not called to be perfect, but we are called to be faithful. To show our children what grace looks like between a tired husband and a stressed-out wife. To lead them not just in morning prayers, but in lives so deeply rooted in Christ that faith isn't just a Sunday activity, it's the language of our home.

And when we mess up, which we will (there should be a parenting blooper reel in heaven), that in itself becomes a chance to model repentance and reliance on God's mercy. As 2 Corinthians 12:9 says, '*My grace is sufficient for you, for my power is made perfect in weakness.*' Even in our most chaotic parenting fails and marital misfires, God is at work.

So, yes, modeling Christ in marriage is hard. It's messy, humbling, and sometimes you wonder if anyone's even paying attention while you're trying to explain godly patience with gogurt in your hair. But your kids are watching. And more importantly, so is the God who entrusted them to you.

RAISING THE NEXT GENERATION OF KINGDOM BUILDERS

In recent years, there has been a noticeable shift in how children are being raised, with many experts and observers noting a decline in parental involvement. This trend has raised concerns about the long-term effects on children's development, values, and sense of purpose.

One of the central issues is the increasing percentage of children spending substantial time without direct parental supervision or engagement. According to a 2014 Pew Research Center study, 46% of U.S. two-parent households have both parents working full time, a figure that has steadily increased over the decades. As a result, many children are spending more time alone, with peers, or with digital devices rather than with their parents.

A 2018 survey by Common Sense Media found that American teens average about seven hours of screen time per day, not including time spent on schoolwork. As screen time rises, meaningful parent-child interaction declines. This change limits the time families spend discussing values, discipline, and life guidance, things traditionally learned at home.

Research also indicates a growing cultural issue tied to this disconnect. The American Psychological Association has reported that children today are facing higher levels of anxiety and depression, some of which is linked to the breakdown of family communication and parental involvement. The National Survey of Children's Health also found that only 55% of children live with both biological parents, down from 85% in the early 1960s. Changes in family structure often affect the consistency of parenting and supervision.

Sociologist Christian Smith, in his book 'Soul Searching: The Religious and Spiritual Lives of American Teenagers,' notes that many young people hold vague spiritual beliefs and know little about core biblical teachings, mainly due to a lack of religious conversations and parental guidance. Smith calls this phenomenon 'Moralistic Therapeutic Deism,' which emphasizes being a good person without deep religious conviction, reinforcing the idea that children form beliefs and morals on their own, or through peer and media influence rather than through parent-guided instruction.

This detachment from parental guidance, according to critics, is contributing to a generation that lacks respect for authority and struggles with a sense of purpose. In his 2019 work, '*The Coddling of the American Mind*,' Jonathan Haidt notes a cultural shift in which young adults are more dependent on feelings than principles when making decisions, a potential result of inadequate formative training in critical moral and spiritual thinking during childhood.

Unfortunately, the combination of economic pressures, fractured family structures, over-reliance on technology, and a weakened cultural emphasis on spiritual and moral teaching has led to a climate in which many children are essentially raising themselves. This trend has implications for a generation that may grow up lacking clear direction, strong values, and a sense of enduring purpose.

On the flip side, as Christian parents, we are called to shape the hearts, minds, and spirits of our children, raising them to become kingdom-minded world-changers. The Bible provides a clear model and numerous exhortations for how we are to carry out this responsibility. At the heart of this calling is the understanding that children are a gift and stewardship from the Lord, and that faithful parenting is a vital means for advancing His kingdom on earth.

1. **Children Are a Heritage from the Lord** - Psalm 127:3 says,

'*Children are a heritage from the Lord, offspring a reward from him.*' This verse reminds us that our children are not simply our own, but a legacy and trust given to us by God. Therefore, the way we raise and educate them has eternal significance. We are called not only to provide for their physical well-being but most importantly to cultivate their spiritual formation.

2. **Parents Are the Primary Disciplers** - One of the most precise instructions is found in Deuteronomy 6:6-7: '*These commandments that I give you today are to be on your hearts. Impress them on your children. Talk about them when you sit at home and when you walk along the road, when you lie down and when you get up.*'

This shows that discipleship is not a passive or occasional activity — it's a lifestyle. Parents are called to be intentional in integrating God's Word into everyday life. This rhythm of teaching, reminding, modeling, and praying with our children lays a robust foundation for kingdom living.

1. **Teach Your Children God's Ways Early** - Proverbs 22:6 exhorts, '*Train up a child in the way he should go; even when he is old he will not depart from it.*' This is both a promise and a principle. Early formation is essential. The values, biblical truths, and God-centered worldview we instill in our children from a young age are seeds that grow with them and shape their decisions, character, and purpose.

2. **Do Not Provoke, But Train in Instruction** - Ephesians 6:4 commands parents (especially fathers): '*Fathers, do not provoke your children to anger, but bring them up in the discipline and instruction of the Lord.*' This verse balances

the necessity of loving discipline and guidance with the importance of modeling Christ-like behavior. Harshness or negligence leads to rebellion and discouragement, but godly training nurtures strong, purpose-driven spiritual leaders.

3. **The Goal Is to Raise Kingdom Builders** - Our children are not just the future of the church—they are active participants in God's kingdom now. 1 Peter 2:9 reminds believers, '*But you are a chosen people, a royal priesthood, a holy nation, God's special possession, that you may declare the praises of him who called you out of darkness into his wonderful light.*' This includes our children. We disciple them not for comfort or success by worldly standards, but to prepare them to proclaim the Gospel, serve with love, and live counter-culturally with bold faith.

4. **Model the Faith Through Action** - James 1:22 warns us not to listen to the Word merely, but to do what it says. Children imitate what they see. Our faithful obedience, repentance, love, service to others, and passion for the Gospel are often more powerful than any words we say. As Deuteronomy 6 reminds us, the commands should first be on our hearts, then taught to our children.

5. **Pray and Intercede Constantly** - Finally, spiritual formation is not done in our strength alone. We are to partner with God through fervent prayer. 1 Thessalonians 5:17 calls us to '*pray without ceasing.*' Parents are called to be intercessors, covering their children in prayer, asking God for wisdom, discernment, and transformation in their lives through the power of the Holy Spirit.

In a culture that increasingly pulls children toward secular values, self-fulfillment, and moral confusion, the biblical model calls Christian parents to rise up and engage deeply in raising a generation rooted in truth, empowered by grace, and equipped to be agents of change in the world. As we pour God's Word, love, and purpose into our children, they will grow to be the next generation of bold, compassionate world-changers who push back the darkness and advance God's kingdom for His glory.

PARENTING AS AN EXTENSION OF MARITAL UNITY

According to God's design, parenting is not a standalone role; it is an extension of the covenantal unity between a husband and wife. From the very beginning, God made it clear that the union of a husband and wife was meant to be the foundational relationship for the nurturing and raising of children. In short, God didn't just throw children into the mix like a surprise twist in a movie. He built the family structure on a solid foundation: marriage.

When God created Adam and Eve, He designed them to be one flesh (Genesis 2:24). This union was more than physical; it was spiritual, emotional, and purposeful. Unity in marriage reflects the unity of God Himself, Father, Son, and Holy Spirit, and creates the fertile soil where children can be nurtured in love, truth, and security. Think of it like a beautifully synchronized dance (or maybe a three-legged race, depending on the day), if one parent is moving in a totally different way from the other, everyone trips, including the kids.

So when God said in Malachi 2:15, '*Did he not make them one, with a portion of the Spirit in their union? And what was the one God seeking? Godly offspring.*' That verse is powerful. It tells us two things: first, the unity of marriage is Spirit-filled; second, its purpose is to produce and raise godly children. Godly offspring aren't just the result of two people producing children; they are the fruit of two people being spiritually, emotionally, and purposefully unified in parenting. As any parent can tell you, raising kids takes more than just teamwork. It takes shared vision, mutual sacrifice, and a lot of grace.

When a husband and wife are on the same page, children flourish. Their environment reflects the character of God, both His authority and His compassion. The father leads with love and strength (Ephesians 5:25, 6:4), and the mother nurtures with gentleness and wisdom (Proverbs 31:26-28). Together, they model the Gospel through humility, consistency, discipline, and joy. They offer a living testimony of what it looks like to live surrendered to Christ.

But as parents, we all know, unity in parenting isn't easy. Sometimes unity looks like quietly negotiating during a toddler meltdown at Target over who's going to say no this time while they lie on their back, kicking and screaming on the floor. Other times, it looks like disagreeing behind closed doors and then coming out as a united front in front of the kids, like generals forming a battle strategy over spilled juice and tablet time.

The truth is, disunity in parenting confuses children. When mom and dad are not aligned, kids often learn to manipulate, pick sides, or feel insecure. But unity offers clarity, peace, and consistent direction. That alignment gives children greater ease in trusting their parents and, ultimately, trusting God. It helps them internalize values, respect authority, and feel deeply loved.

Moreover, when children see their parents loving one another well, forgiving each other, praying together, and facing challenges side by side, it gives them a living picture of faith in action. The home becomes a training ground for the next generation of disciples, rooted in the soil of relational oneness.

So parenting is not a solo mission, nor is it simply a tag-team sport; it is kingdom work borne out of covenant love. It is a daily decision to raise children together while clinging to Christ, remaining unified even during the chaotic dinner hour or while mediating teen drama. God calls us not to be perfect parents, but to be faithful from a place of unity, love, and truth.

When spouses stay aligned on God's Word and dependent on His Spirit, they can reflect His beauty and strength not only to their children but to the watching world. And that is a powerful testimony indeed.

Marriage as a Mission – Reflection & Action Guide
Reflection Questions

1. What message are your kids (or spiritual children) learning about God from your marriage?
2. Do you parent more as individuals or as a united team?
3. How could your marriage more clearly model Christ to your children?

Mission in Action

- Pray with your children as a couple at least once this week.
- Write a short "family mission statement" rooted in Scripture.
- Model unity in front of your kids by making one decision together this week, rather than separately.

Resources:

Smith, Christian, and Amy Adamczyk. *Handing Down the Faith: How Parents Pass Their Religion on to the Next Generation*. Oxford University Press, 2021.

National Study of Youth and Religion (NSYR). University of Notre Dame, directed by Christian Smith, 2001–2005. For data and reports, see: https://youthandreligion.nd.edu/

Pew Research Center. 'Raising Kids and Running a Household: How Working Parents Share the Load.' November 4, 2015. https://www.pewresearch.org/social-trends/2015/11/04/raising-kids-and-running-a-household-how-working-parents-share-the-load/

Common Sense Media. 'The Common Sense Census: Media Use by Tweens and Teens.' 2019. https://www.commonsensemedia.org/research/the-common-sense-census-media-use-by-tweens-and-teens-2019

American Psychological Association. 'Children's Mental Health.' Accessed 2023. https://www.apa.org/topics/children

National Survey of Children's Health. Data Resource Center, Child and Adolescent Health Measurement Initiative. https://www.childhealthdata.org/learn-about-the-nsch/NSCH

Smith, Christian, with Melinda Lundquist Denton. 'Soul Searching: The Religious and Spiritual Lives of American Teenagers.' Oxford University Press, 2005.

Haidt, Jonathan, and Greg Lukianoff. 'The Coddling of the American Mind: How Good Intentions and Bad Ideas Are Setting Up a Generation for Failure.' Penguin Press, 2018.

8. Hospitality as Ministry

When most people hear the word 'hospitality,' they think of cookie-cutter smiles, Pinterest-perfect potlucks, or the art of balancing a deviled egg on a flimsy paper plate without dropping it on your guest's new suede boots. But biblical hospitality? That's a whole different ballgame, less about matching tableware and more about opening your life, your home, and sometimes your last loaf of bread to someone who might be an angel in disguise (see: Hebrews 13:2 and proceed with caution the next time a stranger rings the doorbell).

One of the most striking, and frankly, slightly awkward, examples of hospitality as ministry comes from none other than Father Abraham. You know the story. Abraham is chilling out by his tent, probably enjoying a quiet afternoon in the shade, when three travelers stroll up. Does he send them away because he's still in his bathrobe? Nope. Instead, he springs into action like an ancient Near Eastern Martha Stewart, rushing around to prepare a feast and offer rest. What he doesn't realize at the moment is that one of those guests is the Lord Himself, and the other two are heavenly companions, possibly packing serious angelic credentials!

That dusty roadside lunch became a divine appointment.

Abraham didn't just host guests — he hosted God. No pressure or anything!

This chapter explores how, even in our cluttered homes and cluttered schedules, hospitality can become a powerful ministry. Whether it's sharing a meal or simply making someone feel like they belong, the sacred act of welcoming others can open doors not just to your home, but to the heart of God. And who knows? The person drinking your last cup of coffee might just be sent straight from heaven. So maybe keep that bathroom clean just in case!

USING YOUR HOME AS A PLACE OF MISSION

Our homes are more than just places to collapse after a long day, where socks mysteriously vanish, and the fridge is always one step away from being empty. According to God's design, our homes are meant to be mission outposts, tiny embassies of the Kingdom where love is lived out, hospitality flows freely, and hurting hearts find refuge.

From the very beginning, God has emphasized the importance of hospitality. In fact, hospitality is woven deeply through the biblical narrative. In Romans 12:13, Paul instructs believers to 'share with the Lord's people who are in need. Practice hospitality.' Not a suggestion. Not a Pinterest challenge. A directive. Hospitality isn't about entertaining; it's about ministering. When we open our doors to others, we're opening a window into the love of Christ.

Take the story of the widow at Zarephath in 1 Kings 17. She had barely enough flour and oil to make one last pitiful pancake for herself and her son, and then she expected to die of starvation. Cheery stuff, right? Enter Elijah, the prophet, who strolls into town and essentially says, 'Hey, could you share that last hotcake with me?' Miraculously, she says yes. And because of her hospitality and obedience, not only does the jar of flour never run dry, but she also ends up on the divine A-list of unexpected Bible heroes. That's God's math: give the little you have, and He'll bless it beyond measure.

Around the world, this kind of open-hearted living is often the norm rather than the exception. In countries like Ethiopia, Pakistan, and the Philippines, it's not uncommon for strangers to be invited in for a hot meal and a place to rest, even when the hosts have very little to offer. People may not have a guest room, but they'll offer their own beds or clear a spot on the floor. There's an unspoken understanding that the warmth of a home is meant to be shared.

Contrast that with our Western tendency to treat our homes like fortresses, guarded by security systems, privacy fences, and a general fear of unannounced doorbell rings. (Admit it: if someone shows up without texting first, we dive for cover like we're in a spy movie!) But Scripture calls us to something higher. Hebrews 13:2 urges us not to forget to show hospitality to strangers, '*for by so doing some people have shown hospitality to angels without knowing it.*'

Your home doesn't have to be spotless. Your cooking doesn't need to impress someone named Bobby Flay. What matters is the posture of your heart. When you set a chair at your table, pour a cup of coffee, or offer someone your listening ear, you're doing more than being polite. You're offering the presence of Jesus in a world that desperately needs it.

One powerful real-life story of hospitality leading to blessing and a history-making impact is that of Millie Dienert, affection-ately known as the 'First Lady of Evangelism.' Millie and her husband Carl were a young couple in Pennsylvania when they were introduced to a young preacher named Billy Graham. At the time, Billy was relatively unknown, traveling with a small team of evangelists, living on a shoestring budget, and in need of places to stay.

Millie opened up her home to Billy and his team, not just for one night, but frequently, offering meals, bedrooms, and the warmth of a Christ-centered home. She didn't do it for recognition or because she had plenty to offer. In fact, Millie often shared how humble their resources were in the early days, but their hearts were open. They prayed with the team, encouraged them, and gave them a space to rest and refocus.

What she may not have known at the time was that one of those home-cooked meals shared around her kitchen table was fueling what would become a global evangelistic movement. Billy Graham later became one of the most influential evangelists in history, preaching to over 215 million people in more than 185 countries.

Millie herself later became a powerful voice for the gospel, leading Bible studies and speaking at national prayer breakfasts and Graham crusades. Her legacy grew, and it all began with an open door and a willing heart.

The ripple effect of Millie's hospitality cannot be overstated. She didn't set out to make history; she just made dinner. But her willingness to host a stranger, and eventually a friend, became part of a story much bigger than her own. This is a modern example of Hebrews 13:2 in action: entertaining strangers, not knowing the extent of what God might do through that simple act of kindness.

It just goes to show, you never really know who you're welcoming when you invite someone in for a meal. It might be the next world-changing evangelist... or at least someone who desperately needs to experience the love of Jesus through your casserole. Either way, it's holy ground.

So whether your home has a white picket fence or peeling wallpaper, it can still be a powerful place of mission. After all, some of the greatest ministries in history have started around kitchen tables, not conference stages. Keep the coffee warm and the front door open; Kingdom work might walk in at any moment.

WELCOMING OTHERS: FROM SMALL GROUPS TO NEIGHBORS

Another powerful way we can faithfully steward our homes as a ministry tool is by opening our doors for small groups and inviting our neighbors into genuine fellowship. While Sunday services are a core part of the church experience, the reality is that real spiritual growth often happens in circles, not just in rows. Small groups transform a big church into an intimate, connected community where people not only learn more about God's Word but also learn more about each other.

Anyone who's ever been a part of a large church knows that it can sometimes feel a little...well, large. You might sit next to someone for months without ever learning their name. But something beautiful happens when people step into a living room, grab a seat on the sofa, and open the Word of God together. A small group is where faces become family, and where pew neighbors turn into prayer partners.

This model of meeting in homes is not new; it's actually ancient. Think ancient Jerusalem old! The early church in the book of Acts gives us a fantastic blueprint for this. Acts 2:46-47 says, 'They broke bread in their homes and ate together with glad

85

and sincere hearts, praising God and enjoying the favor of all the people.' These were not grand cathedrals or rented auditoriums; these were kitchens and courtyards, where believers gathered to worship joyfully and support one another through every season of life.

Hosting a small group doesn't mean you need a spotless house or a theology degree. What matters is the environment of openness and authenticity. When people gather in small groups, whether to study Scripture, pray, talk about life, or share a meal, powerful things can happen. It's a sacred mix of vulnerability, encouragement, and accountability. The struggles we often keep hidden in a crowd can be brought into the light in a smaller circle, where grace, wisdom, and support can flow freely.

And it's not just about what you receive, it's also about what you give. Small groups are a powerful way to pour into others. Maybe you're the one who's weathered a tough season and came out stronger. Your story could be the encouragement someone else desperately needs. Maybe it's offering consistent prayer, a listening ear, or even just coffee and cookies. Ministry doesn't always look like preaching a sermon. Sometimes, it looks like folding chairs, open Bibles, and laughter around a kitchen table.

In a world that's lonelier than ever, the Church has an opportunity to offer real community — one living room at a time. So don't underestimate the sacredness of your sofa and snacks. God can use your home not just as a place to live, but as a place to help others come alive in Christ. When you open your doors, you open new doors to discipleship, healing, and friendship, and in turn, you become an embodiment of the early church's heartbeat: growing together, house by house, heart by heart.

Opening our homes for small groups and meaningful fellowship isn't just a nice option; it could be preparation for what's to come. While we currently enjoy the freedom to gather in churches, worship publicly, and practice our faith out loud, Scripture warns that such freedom may not always be guaranteed.

Jesus himself tells us in Matthew 24 that in the last days, many will fall away, and persecution of believers will increase. We're already beginning to see the tightening of religious freedoms in various places around the world, and it's not unrealistic to believe that the global Church could one day be forced underground again. History shows us that when persecution hits, the Church doesn't die — it thrives in unexpected places. And more often than not, those places are homes.

In China, Iran, North Korea, and other countries where Christianity is aggressively persecuted, the Church survives and even grows through secret home gatherings. In these nations, believers risk everything to meet together behind closed doors, studying the Word, praying boldly, and praising quietly. Their courage is breathtaking, and their houses have become where revival is born, not in steeples or stadiums, but around humble tables and in hidden rooms.

The early Church in Acts faced this kind of persecution, too. They met in homes, not because it was cozy, but because it was necessary for survival and spiritual growth. Acts 5:42 says, '*Day after day, in the temple courts and from house to house, they never stopped teaching and proclaiming the good news that Jesus is the Messiah.*' As the outside world grew increasingly hostile, the inside of the home became sacred ground — a sanctuary.

What we are doing now, inviting neighbors over, leading Bible studies in our living rooms, and praying with families at the dinner table, is more than ministry. It's practice. This is our training ground. Learning how to pastor one another through Scripture, to build up believers through encouragement, and to create spiritual refuge in ordinary spaces will prepare us if and when public gatherings become dangerous or forbidden.

More importantly, revival doesn't need a platform — it just needs willing hearts. Throughout history, revivals haven't always started with preachers in pulpits; they've begun with prayer warriors in kitchens, broken people around fireplaces, and worship happening between four walls filled with faith. When the gospel is alive in our homes, it cannot be stopped by locked doors or legislation.

So don't see your small group as just a Sunday night routine or a cozy get-together. See it as a Kingdom strategy. See your home as a mission base. And realize that when we gather even just two or three in Jesus' name, whether in freedom or under pressure, He is there (Matthew 18:20). In your home, revival can begin. And one day, it might be what helps keep the fire of faith alive when the world tries to snuff it out.

MARRIAGE AS A PLATFORM FOR OUTREACH

It all comes full circle when we understand that our homes are more than four walls and a mortgage; they are divine tools in God's hands, and at the center of that home is the covenant of marriage. As Christian husbands and wives, we are called not just to live out the gospel privately, but to model it publicly and minister together as one. Marriage isn't just for our personal happiness; it's a partnership that reflects Christ and the Church, and our home becomes the stage where that beautiful picture is on display for others to see.

When we open our homes, we aren't just offering a place

to sit, we're inviting people into a living testimony of God's grace. Whether it's leading a small group, having neighbors over for dinner, or providing a safe space for someone needing encouragement, our marriages and homes can radiate the love of Christ in tangible ways. People should walk in and feel peace, generosity, laughter, and humility, not because we have it all together (spoiler alert: we don't), but because God is the center of what we've built.

And let's be honest, hospitality as a couple is a ministry all its own. It requires teamwork, prayer, and a shared mission. One might be the host with a gift for conversation, while the other is the mastermind behind the chili in the crockpot. But together, you create an environment where ministry flows naturally from partnership. Your unity becomes your witness.

We must also remember that we didn't get our homes or anything else by our own doing. Deuteronomy 8:18 reminds us that it's God who gives us the ability to produce wealth. Everything we have, including the roof over our heads, comes from Him. That means our homes aren't just blessings to enjoy, they are resources to steward. And the best way to honor God with what He has given us is to use it for His glory and for the good of others.

When we view our homes and marriages through this lens, everything changes. The dinner table becomes an altar. The living room becomes a sanctuary. The marriage becomes a ministry. And the ordinary becomes extraordinary when placed in the hands of an extraordinary God!

So whether you're hosting a Bible study, inviting a neighbor over for coffee, or simply offering a safe space for someone to be seen and heard, remember this: your home and your marriage can be ground zero for revival. It's not about perfection — it's about obedience. And when we say yes to using our homes for ministry, we're saying yes to being part of God's mission, right where we are.

Marriage as a Mission — Reflection & Action Guide
Reflection Questions

1. What holds you back from inviting others into your home?
2. Who in your life right now could benefit from your hospitality?
3. How does your marriage reflect Christ's welcome to others?

Mission in Action

- Invite someone over for coffee, a meal, or fellowship this month.
- Identify one way your home can serve as a place of ministry (e.g., Bible study, mentoring, or meals).
- Pray together for God to bring people across your path to welcome.

9. Work, Calling, and Shared Purpose

I f you've ever woken up on a Monday morning, stared at your alarm clock like it's your sworn enemy, and wondered if your job was devised by someone who hates joy, you're not alone! For many of us, work can sometimes feel like a relentless loop of meetings that could've been emails and emails that should've just disappeared. But what if we've been looking at the whole idea of work the wrong way? What if your job, yes, even that one with the awkward break room and temperamental printer, is actually a calling?

It's tempting to separate faith from work, to assume that real ministry only happens on the mission field, in a church pew, or in between guitar chords at a worship night. But scripture paints a different picture. Throughout the Bible, from the tent-making apostle Paul to the shepherd boy turned king David, God has always worked through people's everyday labor to fulfill His divine purposes. That means your spreadsheet expertise, customer service charm, or the ability to fix a leaky pipe in under ten minutes isn't just useful, it's sacred.

Work isn't just a way to pay bills; it's one of the primary ways God invites us into partnership with Him. He doesn't ask us to clock in to survive, but to thrive with intention. Your job is part of a larger story, one in which God is actively redeeming the world, and He's using people like you to do it. Not just pastors, missionaries, or those folks who seem to radiate peace while managing toddlers, everyone has a role, no matter their job title.

It's easy to underestimate the divine potential of what we do from nine to five. After all, no burning bushes appeared in the office supply closet last time you checked. But purpose doesn't always arrive with flashing lights and choirs of angels. More often, it sneaks in through small acts of faithfulness, being kind to a difficult coworker, pursuing excellence in your tasks, or offering a listening ear to someone who really needs it. These moments may not make headlines, but they echo in eternity.

And let's not forget humor. God certainly has one; look at the duck-billed platypus or the average group chat. We need to approach our work with a measure of lightheartedness, too. That spreadsheet mishap? A lesson in humility. That weirdly specific coffee order your boss insists on? An exercise in patience and character development. While the workplace may not always feel holy, God can create holy moments out of seemingly ordinary ones.

In a world that constantly preaches success as visibility and climbing the corporate ladder, God invites us into something deeper — service. What would your work look like if you saw it less as an obligation and more as an offering? How might your attitude change if today's assignment were actually heaven-sent?

This chapter challenges the idea that our jobs are secular spaces meant for compartmentalization. Instead, you'll discover how work becomes a divine partnership, a place where calling and purpose intersect with spreadsheets and service calls. It's time to reclaim work, not as punishment post-Eden, but as a powerful avenue for kingdom impact.

So whether you're behind a desk, in a classroom, on a construction site, or wrangling toddlers at home (which may actually be the most challenging job of all), remember: you're not just showing up for a paycheck. You're stepping into a purpose-fueled calling with eternal implications. And there's nothing ordinary about that!

INTEGRATING FAITH AND WORK

Integrating faith and work is essential for believers because it reflects the integrity of a life committed to God, honors His lordship over every area of our lives, and serves as a witness to others. Biblically, God never intended a separation between the sacred and the secular; rather, He desires that our faith permeate every aspect of our lives, including our work.

Genesis shows that work was part of God's original design. In Genesis 2:15, it says, '*The Lord God took the man and put him in the Garden of Eden to work it and take care of it.*' This demonstrates that work itself is a good gift, part of our created purpose. Work is not a result of the fall but was sanctified from the beginning. Therefore, integrating faith and work is about aligning our purpose with God's greater plan in everyday tasks.

Colossians 3:23-24 states, '*Whatever you do, work at it with all your heart, as working for the Lord, not for human masters, since you know that you will receive an inheritance from the Lord as a reward. It is the Lord Christ you are serving.*' This passage clearly shows why integrating faith and work is essential: we are not just working for worldly bosses, but for the Lord. Our workplace becomes a platform for worship when we approach it with the mindset that it's ultimately for God.

93

Additionally, in Matthew 5:14-16, Jesus says, '*You are the light of the world. A town built on a hill cannot be hidden… let your light shine before others, that they may see your good deeds and glorify your Father in heaven.*' This means our faith should be visible in how we act and work. When we display honesty, diligence, patience, and love at work, we reflect Christ to others, many of whom might never attend a church or read a Bible.

Take the example of Daniel. Although he lived in a foreign land and served under pagan kings, he integrated his faith with his work. Daniel 6:4 tells us that '*they could find no corruption in him, because he was trustworthy and neither corrupt nor negligent.*' Even when it was risky, Daniel did not compromise his faith; he prayed faithfully, even when laws forbade it. His integrity and faithfulness impressed even King Darius, who eventually acknowledged the power of Daniel's God. Daniel's workplace became the setting for divine influence because he brought his faith into it.

Modern believers can do the same. Consider a Christian woman working as a manager in a secular company. She treats her team with kindness and fairness, avoids gossip, and works diligently without seeking credit. Her behavior stands out, prompting her coworkers to ask why she behaves differently. Over time, she builds trust and shares how her relationship with God shapes her values. Her workplace becomes her mission field.

Integrating faith and work is vital because God designed work as a venue for honoring Him, growing in character, and witnessing to others. Scripture repeatedly supports the idea that our faith should influence every activity, including our jobs. When we work with integrity, excellence, and with a heart of service, we reflect God's kingdom and invite others to notice

His presence in our lives.

There was a time in my life when I worked at LKQ Auto Salvage, about 30 minutes from where I currently work. I spent nine years there, and during that time, I was one of only two people in the entire place who went to church. The environment was rough, to say the least. The men I worked with were tough, gritty, and used to a lifestyle filled with foul language and sharing inappropriate materials like pornography. It was almost their culture that bonded them during break times and in conversations.

When I first started, I stood out. I didn't join in on their conversations. I didn't laugh at crude jokes. I didn't pass judgment loudly or preach at them — I just lived my faith. I did my job honestly, avoided the gossip, showed respect, and prayed silently over my workday. At first, they didn't quite know what to make of me. But over time, they noticed. They paid attention to the kind of man I was and the faith I lived. Eventually, many of them began to keep their language and content away from me. They even started to respect me for the way I lived — not with scorn, but with a quiet recognition that I was different.

I never imagined the full impact of my quiet faithfulness during those nine years. But a few years after I had moved on from LKQ, I received a phone call I will never forget. It was one of the toughest guys I had worked with, a man who always carried himself with strength but also had a hidden kindness. He was in the middle of a family crisis and didn't know where to turn. He told me that when things got bad, his mind went back to the time we had worked together. He remembered how I carried myself, how I was different because of my faith, and in that moment of desperation, he reached out.

He asked me to pray for him and his family. I did, and God answered those prayers. Not long after, he gave his life to Christ and started attending church full-time, where he now lives. His life took a new turn, one filled with hope and faith. And all of it began with a seed planted in a harsh workplace by someone living out their walk with integrity and love, without fanfare.

This experience reinforced to me the importance of integrating our faith and our work. As Colossians 3:23-24 says, we are to work as unto the Lord, not just for human masters. Being faithful in our daily work, even in environments that challenge us spiritually and morally, can have eternal consequences. If I had conformed to the culture there or remained silent about my faith through my actions, this man might never have thought of me in his time of need. Living our testimony matters, not just for ourselves, but for the destinies God wants to shape through us.

I want to be clear that I am not perfect by any means. Like everyone, I have my own struggles, shortcomings, and areas where I still fall short. I've made mistakes, and I constantly rely on God's grace and mercy in my life. But that's what makes it all the more humbling and powerful, that even in my brokenness, God chose to use me.

When I look back on my time working at LKQ, I realize that it wasn't about me being some spiritual giant. I didn't have all the correct answers or live a flawless life. I was trying to be faithful in the place God had put me, to work hard, stand for what is right, and represent Christ in an environment that desperately needed light.

What amazes me is that God can take someone flawed like me and still use my life to impact others. The fact that a former coworker, one of the roughest and kindest individuals I knew, remembered something different about me and reached out years later for prayer, and then came to know Christ, humbles me deeply. It shows that our influence isn't about being perfect; it's about being available and obedient.

God doesn't wait for us to be perfect before He uses us. In fact, He often uses the most unlikely people, those who live with integrity, show kindness, and quietly reflect His love, to bring hope and transformation to others' lives. I'm so thankful that God, in His grace, used my life in that place, and I pray He continues to do so wherever I go.

SUPPORTING EACH OTHER'S CALLINGS

There was a woman named Sarah who had always felt a deep calling from God to serve in ministry. Ever since she was young, she had a heart for women's outreach and dreamed of one day leading a ministry to help broken and hurting women find healing through Christ. After marrying her husband, Mark, she assumed they would share each other's dreams and support one another's callings.

But as the years went by, it became clear that Mark did not understand or support Sarah's calling. He wasn't opposed to ministry, but he was uncomfortable with the time and emotional energy she invested in it. He often made comments like, 'You should focus more on the house and kids,' or 'Do you really think you're the right person for that kind of work?' His lack of encouragement and passive resistance slowly discouraged her.

Sarah continued pushing forward for a while, believing that if she stayed faithful, Mark would come around. She would attend meetings and events, trying to help women, but her heart sank every time she returned home to Mark's disapproval

97

or dismissiveness. Over time, she began to feel torn between honoring her husband and answering God's call. Eventually, the tension in their marriage grew because Sarah felt she was slowly dying inside by not walking fully in God's purpose, and Mark felt neglected and threatened by something he didn't understand.

Their relationship became marked by distance, silent resentment, and unmet expectations. Sarah's passion dimmed, and Mark became bitter, not realizing that by denying her calling, he was not protecting their marriage but slowly damaging the bond they had.

The story illustrates a sobering truth: when one spouse suppresses the other's God-given calling instead of supporting it, both partners suffer. God often places unique callings on each spouse, and mutual support is vital. In Matthew 19:6, Jesus said, '*So they are no longer two, but one flesh. Therefore, what God has joined together, let no one separate.*' That union is meant to include standing together in purpose and calling.

When spouses reject each other's calling, they limit God's work not only in each other's lives but also in their own. Conversely, when they support one another, even in callings they may not fully understand, they both grow, and God is glorified. Support doesn't always mean complete agreement or excitement, but it does mean trusting that God is at work and being willing to walk alongside, not stand in the way.

The story of Sarah and Mark is a reminder that marriage is not just about companionship, but partnership in purpose for the kingdom. Ignoring or rejecting your spouse's calling can not only hinder their obedience to God but also erode the very foundation of trust and shared destiny that marriage is meant to be built upon.

As godly spouses, one of our most significant responsibilities is to support each other in the callings God has placed on our lives. Marriage is not just about companionship and shared responsibilities; it is a spiritual partnership. Part of loving our spouse means helping them become the best and fullest version of who God has called them to be, even when it stretches or challenges us.

When God gives a calling, it is not just for the individual but also for the body of Christ. As a spouse, you are the closest person to your partner, and your support can be a powerful encouragement that fuels their purpose. Your words, prayers, and actions can either propel them toward their destiny or hinder them from reaching it.

This is not a time to be selfish, insecure, or controlling. Supporting your spouse in their calling requires humility and trust in God. It means laying aside personal fears or preferences to align with what the Lord is doing in their life. If we let our own comfort take priority over God's plan, we risk becoming an obstacle instead of a help.

The truth is, if we continually interfere with the design God has placed on our spouse's life, through discouragement, criticism, or withholding support, we may one day be held accountable for the role we played in stifling that calling. Not only will our spouses suffer from unfulfilled potential, but we may also find our own marriage depleted of the joy and passion that comes when both partners walk boldly in their divine purpose.

Romans 12:6 says, '*We have different gifts, according to the grace given to each of us.*' This includes your spouse. When we recognize that our spouse's purpose is a part of God's kingdom plan, we understand that it is holy and worthy of our support, even if the journey looks different from what we imagined.

99

Supporting your spouse's calling is a beautiful way to honor God, strengthen your relationship, and help bring the light of His purpose into the world. It is not about standing in front of them or dragging behind, but walking beside them, believing in what God has called them to do.

I want to point back to the earlier story of Sarah and Mark; the outcome could have been drastically different if Mark had chosen to support Sarah in her calling.

If Mark had taken the time to truly listen to Sarah's heart, to pray with her, and to ask God for understanding and wisdom regarding her purpose, it could have drawn them closer together instead of pushing them apart. Rather than feeling isolated and torn between honoring her marriage and pursuing her calling, Sarah would have felt empowered and encouraged. Mark's support could have been a safe place for her to step confidently into what God had designed her to do, knowing she was not alone.

Instead of Sarah carrying the burden of her vision alone, they could have shared it. Mark would have been a part of the ministry in his own way, through prayer, counsel, practical support, and even simply in cheering her on. He would have shared in the fruit of Sarah's obedience as women were healed, restored, and drawn to Christ through her ministry. Their marriage could have been strengthened as they united around a common purpose that glorified God.

By backing her in her calling, Mark would also have stepped into his own role as a godly leader and helper in Sarah's life. Ephesians 5:25 tells husbands to love their wives just as Christ loved the church and gave Himself up for her. That kind of sacrificial love encourages purpose, uplifts identity, and makes room for growth. By choosing to uphold Sarah's God-given calling, Mark would have become an instrument of God's affirmation in her life rather than a stumbling block.

Together, they could have seen God move through their marriage as a partnership in the gospel. Their home could have become not just a place of love, but a launching pad for ministry and purpose. And both could have experienced deeper joy and fulfillment, knowing they were walking together in obedience.

When spouses support each other's calling, the ripple effects are powerful, not just for the individuals but for their relationship, their family, and everyone touched by their obedience to God's plan.

STEWARDSHIP OF FINANCES FOR KINGDOM ADVANCEMENT

Finances are one of the most common and serious sources of conflict in marriage. Studies consistently show that financial disagreements are one of the leading causes of marital stress and even divorce. According to a Ramsey Solutions study conducted in 2017, money fights are the second leading cause of divorce, just behind infidelity. They also found that couples who disagree about finances at least once a week are 30% more likely to get divorced than those who disagree less often.

One of the key reasons finances become such a painful issue in marriage is that money is deeply tied to trust, values, and communication. When spouses don't steward their finances in a godly and transparent manner, it opens the door to suspicion, resentment, and division.

For example, if one spouse secretly accumulates debt or hides spending, it creates a breach of trust. The secrecy can feel like betrayal, even if the motive wasn't malicious. It signals a lack of unity, which goes against the oneness God designed for marriage. Amos 3:3 asks, '*Do two walk together unless they have agreed to do so?*' Financial agreements require mutual honesty and shared vision. When that breaks down, so does trust.

Another contributing factor is differences in financial priorities. One spouse may be a spender, the other a saver. If Godly stewardship and mutual agreement are not practiced, those differences can lead to ongoing tension. Ecclesiastes 4:9 says, '*Two are better than one, because they have a good return for their labor.*' This applies to finances as well. When finances are handled as a team, under God's direction, they produce peace and fruitfulness. But when each spouse pulls in a different direction, it leads to confusion and disorder.

God calls believers to steward the resources He entrusts to them with wisdom, discipline, and unity. Proverbs 21:5 says, '*The plans of the diligent lead surely to abundance, but everyone who is hasty comes only to poverty.*' Financial planning, budgeting, saving, and generous giving must be agreed upon by both spouses, seeking God's guidance together.

A real-world example might be couples burdened by credit card debt because one partner makes large purchases without discussing them with the other. What starts as financial strain often snowballs into emotional disconnect and conflict. One spouse may feel controlled, while the other feels disrespected. This isn't just a money issue; it becomes a relationship issue because of the breach in communication and trust.

On the other hand, when couples bring their finances before God, pray about financial decisions, and are transparent and accountable with each other, it fosters trust and unity. It becomes an area where they grow spiritually and emotionally.

Finances are deeply connected to marital health. When not

stewarded in a Godly way, with integrity, communication, and shared purpose, they become a source of mistrust and hardship. But when handled according to biblical principles, financial unity can be a powerful testimony of trust, stewardship, and God's faithfulness in marriage.

Sharing finances between spouses is not just a practical consideration; it is a spiritual and relational one. In marriage, two people become one, and that includes financial unity. When spouses do not share or involve each other in household financial matters, it often leads to a breakdown in trust, communication, and accountability.

When one spouse is not fully informed or up to date on the financial status of the marriage, whether it be income, budgeting, debt, or spending, it creates an imbalance. That spouse is left in the dark, unable to make informed decisions or engage with the other in planning and stewardship. This lack of transparency can foster suspicion, misunderstanding, and even resentment. It opens the door to poor accountability, where unchecked spending or secret debt can occur, and when issues arise, it often leads to blame and conflict.

God designed marriage to be a partnership in every area of life, including money. In Genesis 2:24, we read that a man shall leave his father and mother and be united to his wife, and they shall become one flesh. This unity applies directly to the way couples manage their resources. Marriage is not a 50/50 arrangement; it is 100/100, both spouses fully vested and engaged.

When finances are siloed, when each spouse handles money independently or keeps financial matters private, it undermines that oneness. Trust cannot flourish where there is secrecy or a lack of involvement. Even if one spouse is more skilled in budgeting or financial planning, the other should still be informed and engaged regularly. This creates mutual ownership and shared responsibility.

Proverbs 27:23 says, '*Be diligent to know the state of your flocks, and attend to your herds.*' In a marriage context, that means both partners should be diligent in monitoring their household finances. Whether through regular budget meetings, joint planning sessions, or open discussions about spending, being on the same page financially protects the marriage and promotes peace.

Sharing finances encourages accountability. If one partner overspends or financial trouble arises, both are already aware and can tackle the problem together rather than resorting to blame or frustration. It also reflects a deeper commitment to unity, showing that both are working together not only to maintain the household but also to steward God's blessings in a godly way.

God created marriage to strive for unity in all areas, including finances (1 Corinthians 7:4). You don't get to pick and choose which parts of your spouse you want to marry and which parts you don't. Marriage is a full investment; you commit entirely to each other, and this includes the bank accounts.

Recent research supports this idea, showing that couples who share all their finances tend to experience higher levels of relationship satisfaction. The Journal of Personality and Social Psychology notes that partners who pool their money, compared with those who keep some or all of their finances separate, report greater happiness and are less likely to break up.

It's as if God's design proves true.

Of course, different personalities, goals, and financial habits, as well as trust issues, can bring tension. But the response shouldn't be to avoid the problem. Instead, couples should face these challenges together, growing stronger in the process. These financial difficulties are common, and working through them can build a deeper connection.

Dividing finances contradicts God's vision for marriage and is unlikely to lead to deeper satisfaction. Don't fight to separate your money; fight for shared financial unity. Prioritize your marriage over individual financial goals or management preferences. Commit to oneness in every way.

Financial transparency and shared responsibility are essential to a healthy marriage. When both spouses are fully engaged in managing and using their finances, it builds trust, fosters unity, and helps safeguard the marriage from unnecessary conflict and division. Marriage is a team, and that includes being a team with your finances.

Marriage as a Mission – Reflection & Action Guide
Reflection Questions

1. How does your work life impact your marriage — for better or worse?
2. Do you see your finances and careers as separate or unified under God's mission?
3. How can you support each other's callings more intentionally?

Mission in Action

- Review your finances together this week and pray over them as God's resources.
- Write down one way you can encourage your spouse in their

calling this month.

- Pray specifically for God's guidance in using your work and resources for His glory.

Resources:

Ramsey Solutions. (2017). 'Money & Marriage' Study. Ramsey Solutions Research.

Rick, S. I., Garcia-Rada, X., & Olson, K. R. (2023). Pooling finances and relationship satisfaction. Journal of Personality and Social Psychology, 125(5), 680–705. https://doi.org/10.10 37/pspi0000388

Part 4: Overcoming Challenges in the Mission

10. Spiritual Warfare in Marriage

I f you've ever had an argument with your spouse over whether the toilet paper roll should go over or under, only to find yourself questioning the very fabric of your union 20 minutes later, congratulations – you're married! And, whether you realized it or not, you may have just engaged in a tiny skirmish in a much larger, hidden battlefield: spiritual warfare in marriage.

Now, I know what you might be thinking: spiritual warfare? Isn't that for people fighting off demon-possessed dolls in movies or praying for hours in circles in candle-lit rooms? Surely my squabbles over dishes, bills, and the thermostat aren't part of some larger cosmic battle. But let's not be fooled. The enemy of our souls isn't bothered by sensational drama – he's perfectly happy to chip away at a marriage one passive-aggressive comment or misunderstanding at a time.

Marriage, in all its beauty and potential, is ground zero for some of the fiercest spiritual attacks because of what it represents. It's God's design, a reflection of Christ and the Church, a sanctuary for love, unity, service, and growth. So, naturally, it makes sense that the enemy would mark it as a prime target. After all, if he can dismantle a marriage, he can destabilize families, discourage faith, and distort God's image in the world.

But don't worry, this chapter isn't going to be all doom, gloom, and demon talk. In fact, we're going to laugh a little (because we need it), learn a lot, and take some honest looks at the spiritual dynamics that often go unnoticed beneath the surface of everyday married life. We'll uncover how the enemy uses common tactics, lies, discouragement, and isolation to wedge division between two people who were once starry-eyed enough to commit forever.

We'll also take a look at the armor and tools that God has lovingly given us to fight back, not with sarcasm, not with the silent treatment, and definitely not with the dry-erase board that lists who emptied the dishwasher last. But with truth, prayer, unity, humility, and a refusal to let the little foxes spoil the vineyard, as the Song of Solomon so poetically warns.

Because here's the thing: your spouse is not your enemy. Read that again. Make it a fridge magnet. The real enemy loves to make you forget that, turning minor miscommunications into major explosions. Before you know it, you're arguing about laundry hampers when you're really wrestling with deeper issues like fear, insecurity, and unhealed past wounds. But the beauty lies in this: God has not left us to fight alone.

Throughout this chapter, we'll peel back the layers and bring spiritual clarity to the common conflicts. We'll talk about how to recognize when a fight isn't just a fight, and how you can invite God into the ring (spoiler alert: He wins every time). And yes, we'll address what to do when your spouse seems more interested in the remote control than in reconciling after a disagreement. There's grace and guidance for that, too.

So buckle up, and don't worry, this won't be a dry theological lecture. Think of it more like a spiritual boot camp with a good sense of humor, a bit of elbow grease, and a whole lot of Jesus. Consider this your pre-game pep talk. Marriage is not only worth fighting for, but it's also worth fighting well. Let's learn how to do that, together.

RECOGNIZING THE ENEMIES' SCHEMES

Marriage can sometimes feel like a game of whack-a-mole with conflict just when you think you've smoothed out one issue — boom! — Up pops another. It's almost like disagreement and tension are hiding around every corner, waiting patiently to jump out and throw off your whole day (or week). One moment you're both laughing over morning coffee, and the next you're locked in a stare-down over who forgot to take the trash out... again.

Now, it's easy to chalk all this up to relationship quirks and growing pains. And sure, some of it is, we're imperfect people, after all. But what if more often than not, it's not just you two battling each other? What if it's a quiet whisper pushing buttons, poking at pride, and silently sowing seeds of frustration? What if there's something spiritual at play?

This is where it gets real. Satan loves to stir the pot, especially in marriages. He's a master of planting subtle division, wrapping lies in logic, and turning molehills into mountains. He doesn't always come with bells and whistles; sometimes, he nudges us toward suspicion, offense, impatience, or bitterness, and suddenly, you're fighting a battle you think is about laundry but is actually about something deeper.

The goal of the enemy isn't just to start arguments, it's to erode unity. He'd rather see a couple constantly irritated with each other than united in love and purpose. Why? Because two people joined together in Godly strength are a threat to darkness. But two people distracted by petty arguments and silent treatments? That's an easy win for him.

It's not about blaming the devil for everything; sometimes, we wake up on the wrong side of the bed. But we do need to have spiritual eyes to see when a pattern of conflict feels more like sabotage than coincidence. When issues repeat without resolution, when peace feels forced, or when every minor disagreement feels bigger than it should be, it might be time to recognize the fingerprints of spiritual interference.

And here's the trickiest part: Satan doesn't need a full-on crisis to start working against your marriage. He prefers the little things. The cold shoulder. The eye-roll. The missed 'I love you.' These small moments, left unchecked, turn into walls. And walls in marriage don't just separate bedrooms; they separate hearts.

But the good news is, we're not powerless. Not even close. God offers spiritual wisdom and weapons: prayer, humility, forgiveness, Scripture, and the presence of the Holy Spirit to expose lies and bring peace. When we recognize the real battle, we stop fighting each other and start fighting for each other, as teammates, not opponents.

So the next time you feel like you're suddenly butting heads for no good reason, pause. Ask yourself: Is this really about the dishwasher, or is there an invisible hand gently pushing us apart? With awareness and God's help, you can disarm those spiritual sneak attacks before they take root and fight for a marriage that stands firm in truth and love.

Satan is subtle, strategic, and very patient. He doesn't need to come crashing into a marriage with obvious destruction; he's completely content working behind the scenes with slow erosion. Here are some of the most common tactics and schemes he uses to attack marriages:

1. **Division through miscommunication** - One of Satan's favorite ways to drive a wedge between spouses is by warping communication. A simple comment can be misinterpreted, a tone can be misunderstood, or a word can cut deeper than intended. The result? Offense takes root, pride gets in the way of reconciliation, and what could have been cleared up with a quick, humble conversation becomes a days-long cold war.

2. **Isolation** - Satan works hard to isolate each spouse, emotionally, spiritually, and even physically. He whispers things like, 'They'll never understand you,' or 'You're better off keeping this to yourself.' Slowly but surely, isolation grows, and intimacy fades. When you're no longer vulnerable with your spouse, you've handed the enemy a foothold.

3. **Distraction and busyness** - He loves to keep couples so busy and distracted that they stop prioritizing their relationship. Work demands, kids' activities, scrolling for hours on phones, all of it creates distance. When couples stop investing intentional time and energy into each other, the relationship is more vulnerable to dissatisfaction and temptation.

4. **Temptation and comparison** - Whether it's the lure of another person, longing for a more 'ideal' relationship seen on social media, or simply fantasizing about a different life, Satan knows how to bait unfulfilled desires. He uses comparisons to breed discontent and tempt hearts away from the marriage covenant.

5. **Unforgiveness and bitterness** - Holding on to past hurts is one of the most effective weapons the enemy has. He loves it when couples refuse to forgive, offering justification for bitterness and quietly poisoning the relationship from within. Over time, unresolved wounds become major fractures in trust and love.

6. **Spiritual apathy** - When a couple stops praying together, stops seeking God individually or as a unit, and neglects their spiritual growth, Satan finds room to work. A spiritually disconnected marriage often lacks the discernment, strength, and unity needed to withstand trials.

So how do you discern whether something is just a 'normal' marriage conflict or a spiritual attack?

Pay attention to the patterns. If disagreements feel unusually intense, constant with no real resolution, or if you find yourselves emotionally disconnected for extended periods with no apparent cause, it might be part of a spiritual attack. Also consider the fruit: Is it leading to unity or division? Growth or bitterness? Peace or chaos? James 3:16 says, 'For where envy and selfish ambition exist, there will be disorder and every vile practice.' That's often a good diagnostic verse to spot spiritual sabotage.

Finally, go to God. Pray for clarity and wisdom. The Holy Spirit is the best discerner of motives and situations. Invite Him into your marriage, not just in crisis but as a daily participant. When you're sensitive to His voice, it becomes much easier to recognize when the enemy is stirring the pot. And when he is, don't panic. Just pick up your spiritual weapons, link arms with your spouse, and fight back together.

PROTECTING UNITY AGAINST DIVISION, BUSYNESS, AND

TEMPTATIONS

Learning to fight Satan and his tactics is not just a Sunday sermon topic — it's a daily battle for every believer. The enemy's number one goal is to divide us, distract us, and derail us from God's purpose. But the good news is, we're not defenseless. We've been given spiritual weapons, and it's time we learn how to use them.

First, we must guard our unity. Satan loves to stir up division in families, in churches, in friendships. He plants seeds of offense, miscommunication, and pride, hoping we'll water them with hurt feelings and let them grow into walls that separate. But unity is powerful. In fact, when believers come together in love and humility, it shakes the gates of hell. To fight division, we have to choose forgiveness, speak the truth in love, and value what unites us more than what divides us.

Next, we need to be on guard against busyness. Yep, Satan doesn't always tempt you with big evil things. Sometimes he keeps you so busy that you forget to be still with God. Overbooked calendars lead to undernourished souls. If the devil can't destroy you, he'll distract you, and nothing distracts like endless tasks and constant pressure. To fight back, we must learn to rest, prioritize time with God, and focus on what truly matters. Jesus wasn't rushing around and changed the world; surely we can slow down, too.

We also need to win the battle over temptation. Satan knows your weaknesses. He customizes temptations like a tailor fits a suit. What's hard for one person isn't hard for another, but whatever your struggle may be, anger, lust, pride, comparison, or gossip, the enemy will offer it, gift-wrapped and sugar-coated. But we fight temptation by filling our hearts with God's

Word. When Jesus was tempted, He didn't argue; He quoted Scripture. We need to do the same. Memorize the truth so you can recognize lies.

The fight against Satan isn't about being perfect; it's about being prepared. With prayer as our weapon, faith as our shield, and love as our battle cry, we can protect unity, resist temptation, and live focused lives that reflect Christ. We're not helpless — we're warriors. So lift your head, tighten your spiritual belt, and don't give the enemy even an inch.

Staying unified in our walk with Christ and standing firm against division, busyness, and temptation takes intentionality, humility, and spiritual maturity. The Bible gives not only commands but also powerful examples and truths to help us walk this path together.

- **Prioritize humility and service to one another** - One of the primary roots of division is pride, thinking we're better, smarter, or more right than someone else. The remedy is humility, modeled perfectly by Jesus.

Philippians 2:3-5 says, '*Do nothing from selfish ambition or conceit, but in humility count others more significant than yourselves. Let each of you look not only to his own interests, but also to the interests of others. Have this mind among yourselves, which is yours in Christ Jesus.*'

Jesus washed His disciples' feet, including Judas (John 13:12-17). In doing so, He showed us that unity is protected when we choose to serve one another, even those who may hurt or misunderstand us.

- **Make space for one another through grace and forgiveness**

- Division grows where unforgiveness lives. Paul exhorted the Colossians in Colossians 3:13-14: '*Bear with one another and, if one has a complaint against another, forgive each other; as the Lord has forgiven you, so you also must forgive. And above all these put on love, which binds everything together in perfect harmony.*'

The unity of the early church thrived when believers chose to extend grace and prioritize love. If we hold on to grudges, Satan gains a foothold (Ephesians 4:26-27).

- **Fight busyness with margin and meaningful time with God** - Jesus, though fully God, made margin for prayer, solitude, and rest. In Luke 5:16, it says, '*But Jesus often withdrew to lonely places and prayed.*' He chose solitude to stay spiritually aligned and to avoid being pulled in every direction.

When busyness controls us, we lose our spiritual sensitivity. The story of Mary and Martha in Luke 10:38-42 shows us that while Martha was '*distracted with much serving,*' it was Mary who chose '*what is better*', sitting at Jesus' feet. Let's not confuse activity for intimacy. Unity in the body is preserved when we are spiritually healthy.

- **Stay accountable to one another in the face of temptation** - Temptation becomes more dangerous in isolation. The enemy loves it when believers battle alone. In Ecclesiastes 4:9-10, it says, '*Two are better than one... if either of them falls, one can help the other up. But pity anyone who falls and has no one to help them up.*'

James 5:16 teaches, '*Confess your sins to each other and pray for each other so that you may be healed.*' Accountability isn't punishment — it's protection.

Joseph in Genesis 39 stood firm against Potiphar's wife's temptation, not because he was lucky, but because he had predetermined who he would honor. Unity thrives when we collectively pursue purity and hold each other up in our weak moments.

- **Stay united through shared purpose and vision** - When we keep our eyes on the mission, the Great Commission, there's less time to argue and more momentum to move forward together.

In Acts 2:42-47, the early believers devoted themselves to teaching, fellowship, breaking of bread, and prayer. As a result, they were united, awed, and experienced daily spiritual growth. They weren't perfect, but their unity was driven by purpose.

Ephesians 4:3 instructs, '*Make every effort to keep the unity of the Spirit through the bond of peace.*' This unity is not automatic; it takes effort, intentional communication, and shared spiritual goals.

To stay unified and resist division, busyness, and temptations, we must pursue humility, grace, accountability, rest, and shared purpose. We fight with spiritual discipline, not human strength. Unity is the atmosphere where God commands His blessing (Psalm 133:1-3), and Satan will do anything to disrupt it. But when the church chooses love over ego, grace over offense, and mission over distraction, we become an unstoppable force for the Kingdom of God.

117

ARMOR OF GOD APPLIED IN MARRIAGE

Marriage is one of the most beautiful gifts from God, and also one of the most significant battlefields for spiritual warfare. The enemy knows that strong marriages reflect God's love and unity, so of course, he tries to attack them with division, busyness, miscommunication, pride, and temptation. Enter: the Armor of God (Ephesians 6:10-18). Not just for individual spiritual battles, but incredibly powerful when applied to marriage. Let's dig into each piece and apply it to married life.

Belt of Truth - This is foundational. Without truth, everything else falls apart. In marriage, wearing the belt of truth means being honest with ourselves and each other. No hiding feelings, no passive-aggressive 'I'm fine' when you're clearly not. Speak the truth in love (Ephesians 4:15). It's about being transparent, not brutal. If your spouse asks if you like that new casserole and it tastes like drywall, try being lovingly honest. 'Well, it's not your finest work, but I'm thankful you made it!' That's the truth with grace.

Breastplate of Righteousness - This protects our hearts, figuratively and biblically. In marriage, it means choosing to live with integrity, guarding your emotional world, and remaining faithful in both your actions and your motives. It's not just avoiding the big sins; it's about keeping your heart right in the daily stuff like choosing not to hold a grudge when your spouse leaves dishes in the sink for the 13th day in a row. Guard your heart, because from it flows the wellspring of your love life and your patience.

Shoes of the Gospel of Peace - These shoes help you carry peace wherever you go, even across the giant chasm between how you load the dishwasher and how your spouse does it

118

(clearly incorrectly). The gospel brings reconciliation. In marriage, that means being the first to say 'I'm sorry,' approaching conflict with humility, and actively working to be peacemakers, not peacekeepers who shove issues under the proverbial rug. When both spouses wear these gospel shoes, forgiveness happens faster, and conflict doesn't turn into a cold war.

Shield of Faith - This one is vital for extinguishing those fiery arrows, things like doubt, lies from the enemy, and insecurities. In marriage, it may look like trusting God when finances are tight, or believing that restoration is possible during a rough patch. When you both hold up this shield, you can remind each other of who God is and what He's promised instead of letting the enemy sow fear, discouragement, or mistrust. Bonus tip: occasionally using the shield of faith to block sarcasm darts might help, too.

Helmet of Salvation - This protects the battlefield of the mind. In marriage, the enemy often whispers lies: 'They don't care about you.' 'You married the wrong person.' 'They'll never change.' The helmet of salvation helps you reject those lies and remember your identity in Christ, and your spouse's identity too. You're both redeemed, chosen, and imperfect people being shaped by Jesus. Having this mindset can be marriage-saving. Remember: your spouse is not your enemy; your real enemy wants you to think they are.

Sword of the Spirit (the Word of God) - This is your only offensive weapon. In marriage, depend on God's Word to guide your actions, resolve conflict, and build hope. When tension rises, instead of digging into your box of zingers, pull out Scripture. For example, instead of saying 'You always ignore me!' say, 'Let's strive to be quick to listen, slow to speak, and slow to anger like James 1:19 says.' Sure, it won't always win the argument, but it may win the heart. A couple that learns to speak and pray Scripture together is a powerful team.

Prayer (the secret sauce) - Though not technically armor, Paul ends by commanding us to pray in the Spirit on all occasions. Praying for each other and with each other is one of the most unifying and spiritually bulletproof actions in a marriage. It's hard to stay mad at someone when you're bringing them before God in prayer every day (though we've all tried). Prayer brings unity, softens hearts, and invites God into the middle of your relationship where He belongs.

The full Armor of God isn't just for storming spiritual castles; it's essential gear for the holy battlefield of marriage. When both spouses commit to putting on their armor daily, shoulder to shoulder, sword and shield ready, the enemy has a much harder time sneaking in. So suit up, laugh often, pray continually, give lots of grace, and remember, you're fighting together, not with each other.

Marriage as a Mission – Reflection & Action Guide
Reflection Questions

1. Where do you see the enemy attacking your marriage most?
2. Do you regularly pray together for protection? Why or why not?
3. How does unity serve as a weapon against the enemy's schemes?

Mission in Action

· Read Ephesians 6:10-18 together.

- Choose one piece of the armor of God to pray over your marriage daily this week.
- Commit to a "no division" week. When conflict arises, pause to pray together before speaking.

11. Resilience Through Trials

Being head-over-heels in love is a beautiful thing — your partner laughs at your weird jokes, brings you snacks without asking, and remembers that you like exactly three ice cubes in your drink. It's all sunshine, dopamine, and matching hoodies. But then comes real life.

Trials, losses, and disappointments, like job loss, a health scare, losing a loved one, or discovering your in-laws plan to move in 'just for a few weeks', can rattle even the most rock-solid relationship. Why? Because during good times, love feels effortless. But when life throws curve balls, those emotional reserves start getting tested... and sometimes depleted faster than your favorite streaming device's battery during a binge-watch session.

You see, love isn't just romantic walks and Netflix cuddles. It's also about partnership in the trenches, navigating financial stress, coping with loss, and managing stress when plans don't pan out. Suddenly, the person you once gazed at dreamily over pancakes is now the same person you're blaming for forgetting to pay the utility bill. Again.

Stress has a funny way of shrinking patience and inflating frustrations. Communication breaks down, assumptions creep in, and what started as a team of two can begin to feel like a boxing match in matching robes. Hurtful words fly, sometimes simply because someone left toothpaste clumps in the sink... but it's never really just about toothpaste, is it?

The key isn't avoiding hardships — that's impossible. It's learning to face them together, not at each other. Couples who weather storms well often communicate openly (without sarcasm becoming a second language), lean on empathy, and sometimes admit, 'Yeah, today was awful, and I'm being a bit of a jerk. I'm sorry.'

Love isn't the absence of storms; it's both partners remembering why they boarded the same boat in the first place, even when the waves hit. And yes, sometimes that includes hugging it out... right after arguing over who took the last cookie!

SUFFERING, LOSS, AND DISAPPOINTMENT

Suffering, loss, and disappointment can deliver a devastating blow to a marriage. While romantic love and commitment may be strong, intense emotional pain from events like the death of a child, a parent's passing, or significant life setbacks can shake the very foundation of a relationship. These events often surface individual coping mechanisms that may not align, leading to miscommunication, emotional distance, or even resentment between partners.

Take the loss of a child, for example — few things are as heartbreaking. It is often referred to as one of the most traumatic experiences a couple can go through. Statistically, studies have shown that married couples who suffer the death of a child face a significantly increased risk of divorce. Some research, including a study published in the journal *Omega -

123

Journal of Death and Dying*, has suggested divorce rates among bereaved parents can range from 70% to 90%. Other studies, like those from The Compassionate Friends, indicate the actual divorce rate is lower, around 16% to 25%, but still elevated compared to the general population.

The discrepancy is due to several variables: the strength of the marriage before the loss, how each partner processes grief, and whether they seek support. Often, grief causes one spouse to retreat inwardly while the other may prefer to talk and connect. This mismatch can lead to clashes and emotional misfires. One spouse might become overly focused on work or distractions to numb the pain, while the other feels lonely and abandoned. What is meant to be a shared journey of healing becomes two parallel paths, and both partners may feel misunderstood or unsupported by the other.

Similarly, when one loses a parent, it can stir unresolved emotional issues, trigger identity questions, or lead to depressive symptoms. If the surviving partner doesn't know how to navigate this or ends up feeling neglected or pushed away, resentment can quietly take root.

And it's not just death. Job loss, infertility, failed life plans, and chronic illness also bring emotional baggage that, if not unpacked respectfully and intentionally, can turn allies into adversaries. According to the Holmes-Rahe Stress Inventory, many of the highest-ranked life stressors are often relationship-centered or loss-related, and high stress correlates with emotional strain in a marriage.

The real danger comes when couples don't talk about their grief or disappointment or treat each other like teammates in pain. When coping strategies turn into avoidance, blame, or withdrawal, marriages can start to unravel.

That's why support is so essential; therapy, grief counseling, peer support groups, or even marital counseling can help couples realign and process their losses together. While suffering may be a part of life, how couples respond to it, openly, compassionately, and with shared vulnerability, can make all the difference between a relationship breaking apart or growing stronger.

When marriages face extreme hardship such as the loss of a loved one, financial collapse, betrayal, or life-altering disappointment, the road to healing can feel impossible. But both Scripture and psychological studies point to hope and practical steps that can help couples move from surviving to rebuilding.

From a biblical standpoint, marriage is viewed as a sacred covenant, not just a contract. In Ephesians 5:25, Paul instructs, '*Husbands, love your wives, just as Christ loved the church and gave himself up for her.*' This verse encourages sacrificial love — the kind that stays when it hurts, listens when it's easier to shut down, and serves even when one feels empty. Equally, Ephesians 4:32 urges, '*Be kind and compassionate to one another, forgiving each other, just as in Christ God forgave you.*' These aren't feel-good verses for Instagram posts — they're hard truths meant to hold couples together when everything else is falling apart.

One of the very best paths forward, especially in the darkest valleys, is choosing to lean in rather than pull away. That includes openly communicating grief, being patient with one another's differences, and committing to walking through the pain together, rather than allowing it to divide.

Biblical counseling emphasizes the importance of prayer, community, and seeking godly wisdom. Proverbs 15:22 says,

'Plans fail for lack of counsel, but with many advisers they succeed.'
Seeking pastoral guidance or godly therapists who are equipped
to handle trauma or grief can significantly help.

From a psychological and sociological perspective, studies
affirm the power of counseling and connection. Research
from the Journal of Marital and Family Therapy suggests that
couples therapy can improve relationships by 70%, especially
when both partners are committed to improvement. Grief
counseling, in particular, can bring clarity and help normalize
the different grieving styles between spouses, which can often
be a significant cause of conflict when not understood.

Furthermore, couples who pray together and share spiritual
practices consistently report higher levels of marital satisfaction and resilience. A study published by the National Institute
of Health found that couples with shared religious beliefs and
practices were more likely to recover from life crises than those
without them.

So, the best path forward involves a combination of spiritual
and practical actions:

1. Commit to unity and keep showing up, even when you're
hurting.
2. Bring your grief, confusion, and hurt before God. Prayer not
only changes things — it changes us.
3. Seek godly counsel from pastors or Christian therapists.
4. Lean on a supportive faith community that can help carry
your burdens, just like Galatians 6:2 tells us: *'Carry each other's
burdens, and in this way you will fulfill the law of Christ.'*
5. Focus on forgiveness, humility, and kindness, foundational
traits that offer healing where words or logic fail.

There is no quick fix for deep wounds, but there's a powerful truth in Romans 8:28: '*And we know that in all things God works for the good of those who love him.*' That includes broken marriages, shattered expectations, and seasons of intense suffering. With intentional faith, emotional honesty, and mutual effort, couples can not only recover from devastating setbacks but experience a deeper, more resilient love than they had before.

HOW HARDSHIP CAN DEEPEN MISSION, NOT DERAIL IT

Most of the time, when we go through hardship, whether it's loss, disappointment, betrayal, or failure, our natural instinct is to withdraw. We start thinking, maybe I heard God wrong... perhaps I'm not called after all... maybe the dream was too big, or too bold. Pain has a way of clouding our vision and turning the volume down on God's promises while turning it way up on fear, doubt, and discouragement.

It's a common human reaction: we believe that if something is truly from God, it should be smooth sailing. But Scripture clearly shows that most of the people God used in powerful ways had to endure intense hardship. Look at Joseph. He had a God-given dream and ended up betrayed by his brothers, thrown into prison, and falsely accused. At any point, he could have said, 'Forget it. It's not worth it.' But he didn't. And eventually, what others meant for evil, God used for good.

The enemy loves nothing more than to use suffering to make us believe that the calling on our life has somehow expired. He wants pain to paralyze us, detour us, convince us that we're disqualified. But the truth is, hardship doesn't cancel your mission — it can refine it. Disappointment doesn't delete God's promises — it can deepen your dependence on Him.

When Paul was shipwrecked, beaten, and imprisoned for sharing the Gospel, he didn't walk away and say, 'Well, clearly, this isn't working out.' He wrote epistles that we're still reading 2,000 years later. When Jesus faced the cross, enduring the most significant suffering imaginable, He didn't give up on His mission — He fulfilled it.

So yes, hardship will tempt us to quit, to protect ourselves, to shrink our dreams, to abandon the purpose God has marked out for our lives. But God never promised the road would be easy. He only promised that we wouldn't walk it alone, and that He would bring beauty from ashes.

If you're in a painful season, don't press the eject button on your calling. Don't let temporary pain lead to permanent abandonment of your mission. Let the hardship train you, not derail you. And remember what Galatians 6:9 says: '*Let us not become weary in doing good, for at the proper time we will reap a harvest if we do not give up.*'

Your breakthrough might be waiting right on the other side of the storm you're tempted to run from.

When we go through trials, it can feel like everything is falling apart: our marriage, our purpose, our faith. But through Scripture, we learn that God's intent in allowing these trials isn't to break us, but to build us. He uses hardship not as punishment, but as preparation. God allows us to walk through these refining fires so we can come out stronger, wiser, and more deeply rooted in Him.

In fact, one of the most powerful truths in the Bible is that God does not waste pain. He uses it to sharpen our character, awaken our purpose, and strengthen our relationships, primarily our marriages. When couples go through difficulties together, God desires to use those moments to bond them more tightly, to teach them grace, patience, and a deeper level of sacrificial love.

James 1:2-4 says, '*Consider it pure joy, my brothers and sisters, whenever you face trials of many kinds, because you know that the testing of your faith produces perseverance. Let perseverance finish its work so that you may be mature and complete, not lacking anything.*' This doesn't mean we enjoy suffering, but we can rejoice knowing that God is working in us and through us during those dark and painful seasons.

Job is another example. He lost everything, his family, his health, his wealth, and in Job 23:10, he declares, '*But He knows the way that I take; when He has tried me, I shall come out as gold.*' Job understood that God wasn't absent in his suffering. He was shaping him, refining him, setting him up for something greater. And sure enough, at the end of Job's story, God restored him and gave him double what he had before.

In marriage, trials come, financial stress, sickness, loss, misunderstandings, but if we allow God, those very trials can be what forges a supernatural strength in the relationship. Romans 5:3-5 says, '*Not only so, but we also glory in our sufferings, because we know that suffering produces perseverance; perseverance, character; and character, hope. And hope does not put us to shame, because God's love has been poured out into our hearts.*'

We sometimes feel abandoned in our pain, especially when we're crying ourselves to sleep or watching our dreams crumble. But God never forgets us. Isaiah 43:2 reminds us, '*When you pass through the waters, I will be with you; and when you pass through the rivers, they will not sweep over you. When you walk through the fire, you will not be burned.*' God doesn't say if, He says when, because trials are part of life. But so is His faithful presence through every single one.

129

These trials are not meant to derail your calling or destroy your marriage — they're intended to deepen your testimony. Marriages founded on Christ and weathered through the storm can become stronger than ever before. And callings refined in suffering carry more weight, more compassion, more power.

So let God use your trial. Let Him strengthen your marriage through it. Let Him refine your purpose and make your life, and your love, shine like gold. Painful seasons may be part of the journey, but with God, they are never the end of the story.

STORIES OF COUPLES WHO GLORIFIED GOD IN STORMS

Here are some examples of couples in the Bible who walked through storms but ultimately glorified God through their lives and faith:

Abraham and Sarah – Faith Through Waiting and Uncertainty

Abraham and Sarah are a powerful example of a couple that weathered deep disappointment and uncertainty. God promised them a child and a great nation that would come from their lineage, yet they waited decades without seeing any evidence. Sarah struggled with doubt and even laughed at the idea of having a child in her old age (Genesis 18:12), while Abraham continued to trust God through many tests, including the ultimate one in Genesis 22. Despite their moments of weakness and human mistakes (like trying to fulfill the promise through Hagar), they ultimately trusted God, and He was faithful. Isaac was born miraculously, and through their lineage came the nation of Israel and, eventually, Jesus Himself. Their story shows that even in delay and instability, faith in God can lead to promises fulfilled and glory to His name.

Ruth and Boaz – Redemption Through Brokenness and Loyalty

Ruth and Boaz's story is not just a love story but a testimony of loyalty, faith, and redemption that emerged from significant loss. Ruth was widowed and chose to stay with her mother-in-law, Naomi, after the death of her husband. Boaz was a righteous man who showed kindness and integrity. Their union came from a place of brokenness, but because they trusted in God, they were used to continue the lineage that would lead to King David and, ultimately, to Jesus (Ruth 4:13-22). They honored God not in a palace, but in the fields, through everyday faithfulness. Their love and marriage glorified God in a season that began with loss.

Priscilla and Aquila – Partnership in Ministry Amidst Persecution

Priscilla and Aquila are a less talked-about couple, but they were spiritual powerhouses in the New Testament. They were tentmakers by trade, like the Apostle Paul, and opened their home for the church (Acts 18:2-3; Romans 16:3-5). They endured persecution and displacement but stayed faithful to God's mission. They taught and discipled others, including Apollos, helping clarify the teachings of Christ (Acts 18:24-26). Their marriage was a true partnership in kingdom work — even in hard times and a hostile environment, they gave everything to Jesus. Together, they glorified God not just through survival, but through courage and bold ministry that impacted the early

Church.

Each of these couples faced hardship, but instead of letting their storms break them, they allowed God to use their lives and their marriages to bring Him glory. Their stories remind us that God is not only present in the storm — He is also able to bring purpose and power through it.

Here are a couple of real-life stories of married couples who glorified God through incredibly difficult seasons in their lives:

Scott and Janet Willis – Trusting God After Unthinkable Loss

In 1994, Scott and Janet Willis from Chicago were traveling with six of their nine children in a minivan when a tragic accident changed their lives forever. A truck in front of them lost part of its load, and a piece of metal flew off and punctured their gas tank. The van burst into flames. All six of their children in the van perished.

A loss of that magnitude would completely crush most people. And there's no denying that Scott and Janet were devastated. But rather than turn away from God, they leaned into Him with deeper trust. In their public statements, Scott said, 'The depth of our pain is indescribable. Yet the Lord has sustained us, and His grace has been sufficient.' They made a covenant not to let this tragedy divide their marriage or their faith.

Through their suffering, Scott and Janet became a living testimony of how God can uphold a couple even in the face of unimaginable grief. They ministered to others who were grieving and continued to trust in God's sovereign purpose, bringing glory to Him through their steadfast faith.

Jeremy and Adrienne Camp – Worship in the Shadow of Loss

Christian musician Jeremy Camp married his first wife, Melissa, knowing that she was battling ovarian cancer. She had strong faith and believed God could heal her, and Jeremy stood by her side in love and support throughout the process. Sadly, just a few months after their wedding, Melissa passed away at age 21.

It was a heartbreaking storm in Jeremy's life, but instead of turning bitter, he picked up his guitar and began to worship God through songs of surrender and trust. One of his most famous songs, 'I Still Believe,' came out of that painful season.

Years later, Jeremy married Adrienne, lead singer of the Christian band The Benjamin Gate. Together, they've continued to glorify God through marriage, parenting, and ministry. They've openly shared Jeremy's story and their journey of redemption and healing, encouraging countless others who have experienced profound loss.

Jeremy and Adrienne's marriage is built on faith and purpose, and they've used every part of their journey, both the tragedy and the healing, to glorify God in concerts, interviews, and through the 2020 film based on their story, also titled 'I Still Believe'.

These couples show that storms don't have to destroy a marriage — they can deepen it. When couples choose to run to God together rather than run apart, their suffering becomes a testimony. In pain, they find purpose. In loss, they find love refined. And in the ashes, they glorify the One who still holds their future.

Marriage as a Mission – Reflection & Action Guide
Reflection Questions

1. What has been the hardest trial your marriage has faced?

2. How did God use that season to strengthen or shape you?

3. How can you prepare now for future storms?

Mission in Action

- Share one past trial and thank God together for His faithfulness.
- Read James 1:2–4 and discuss how trials can grow your faith.
- Write a list of 3 blessings you can hold onto when difficulties arise.

Resources:

Camp, Jeremy, and Ken Abraham. I Still Believe. Tyndale House Publishers, 2003. - I Still Believe. Directed by Andrew and Jon Erwin, performances by K.J. Apa and Britt Robertson, Lionsgate, 2020.

The Willis Family Tragedy. Coverage in multiple news archives, including The Chicago Tribune and Christianity Today, 1994 and following.

Compassionate Friends National Survey. Organization offering grief support after the death of a child. Parenting After the Death of a Child: 2011 Survey.

Rhoades, Galena K., and Scott M. Stanley. 'Relationship Education Research: Current Status and Future Directions.' Journal of Marital and Family Therapy, vol. 40, no. 4, 2014, pp. 507–520.

The Holmes-Rahe Stress Inventory. Developed by Thomas Holmes and Richard Rahe, Journal of Psychosomatic Research, 1967.

National Institute of Health (NIH) studies on shared faith practices and marital resilience.

Worden, J. William. Grief Counseling and Grief Therapy: A Handbook for the Mental Health Practitioner. Springer Publishing Company, 2008.

Wright, H. Norman. Helping Those Who Hurt: A Handbook for Caring and Crisis Situations. Regal Books, 2003.

Part 5: Leaving a Legacy

12. Marriage That Multiplies

Most couples don't wake up in the morning sipping coffee and talking about their legacy. They're usually just trying to figure out who left the laundry in the washer for the third day in a row or who forgot to take the chicken out of the freezer. Legacy? That sounds like something reserved for billionaires with their names etched on hospital wings or ancient knights who battled dragons. But in reality, leaving a legacy is precisely what God expects of us as couples.

Marriage isn't just about being adorable together in Christmas sweaters or taking synchronized selfies on vacation. It's about walking through life hand in hand, building something that lasts beyond our years. God calls couples to be the kind of team that fights for each other, not against each other. He wants us to be remembered not for how cute our wedding hashtag was, but for how fiercely we loved, served, and accomplished things in His name.

He's not calling us to survive our marriages; He's calling us to thrive in them. That means sticking together through the storms, the sock piles, and the burnt dinners, and still saying, 'Yes, we're in this, together, for God's purposes.'

So, while the world may be chasing Instagram-worthy moments, let's be couples chasing impact. Let's be remembered as the duo who didn't just coast through marriage, but stormed through with faith, purpose, and a whole lot of laughter. Because in the end, God's not just keeping track of how happy we were, He's seeing how faithful we were. Now that's a legacy worth leaving.

DISCIPLING YOUNGER COUPLES

As we grow and mature in our marriages, it's easy to settle into a rhythm, date nights require advanced planning, communication becomes smooth(er), and we've figured out which battles are worth fighting (spoiler alert: not the toothpaste cap). But with that experience comes responsibility. Just as Jesus poured into His disciples, sharing wisdom, truth, and humility, we are called to do the same for the younger couples who come behind us.

Jesus didn't walk His journey alone. He intentionally gathered people around Him, taught them, shared life with them, and prepared them to carry on the mission. His model wasn't just about preaching sermons — it was about doing life together. He showed them how to rest, how to pray, how to handle conflict, and even how to deal with people who doubted or betrayed you (because let's be real, every marriage will deal with its share of 'Judas moments').

In the same way, we seasoned couples should look around and ask, 'Who can we walk alongside?' Not because we have it all figured out, trust me, sometimes we're still arguing about who left the car on empty, but because we've learned a few things and have the scars (and prayer journals) to prove it.

Discipling younger couples doesn't mean putting together a PowerPoint presentation on communication techniques. It

138

means inviting them into your real life. Show them how you pray together (even when you're both exhausted and one eye is still open). Let them see how you navigate disagreements without tearing each other down. Be honest about your mistakes and generous with your encouragement.

The legacy of a strong marriage isn't just what we build in our own home; it's also about the seeds we plant in others. So let's follow Jesus' lead. Let's take a few younger couples under our wing, buy them coffee, share our messes and victories, and remind them that God is writing a good story in their marriage, too. Because one day, they'll be the seasoned ones, and hopefully, they'll think back and say, 'We had someone who walked with us. Now it's our turn.'

Discipling a couple isn't about being perfect or having all the correct answers — it's about being intentional, authentic, and available. At its core, it means walking alongside another couple, helping them grow in their relationship with each other and with Christ. It looks a whole lot like real life, sitting at the dinner table, praying together, sharing honest stories of your own struggles and victories. It's not about creating a flawless sermon on marriage; it's about giving them a front-row seat to how God shows up in a real, sometimes messy, sometimes miraculous marriage.

Think of it like spiritual mentorship with a relational twist. It's smiling and saying, 'We've been there too, and we're still choosing each other every day, and here's how you can do it with God at the center.'

Here are some practical ways to disciple a couple and leave a lasting legacy:

1. **Be Available and Approachable:** Open your home and your

lives. Invite them over for dinner or coffee. Let them see how you interact in both peace and conflict. Let them ask the hard questions, and be real in your responses.

2. **Share Your Story:** People relate to transparency more than perfection. Share your journey, the good, the bad, and the grace in between. Let them see how faith has shaped your decisions, parenting, forgiveness, and love.

3. **Pray With and For Them:** There's something powerful about a couple knowing someone is praying for their marriage. Send them a text after they've had a tough week. Pray with them when you meet. Teach them how to pray together as a couple if it's new to them.

4. **Study the Word Together:** Whether it's a marriage-focused book, a scripture study, or simply reading a few verses during your time together, keep the Word central. Remind them they're building on a foundation far stronger than feelings or circumstances.

5. **Encourage Consistency, Not Perfection:** Growth comes in the daily choices to love well, forgive quickly, and seek God faithfully. Encourage them when progress feels slow or when setbacks come. Pour grace over their journey.

6. **Be There for the Milestones and the Mundane:** Cheer them on during promotions, new babies, and anniversaries, but also show up during losses, parenting struggles, or just navigating a tough week. Legacy is built through those small touch points over time.

7. **Challenge Them Toward Purpose:** Help them see their marriage is not just for personal happiness — it's also for kingdom impact. Help them discover how they can serve others, raise children in faith, and be a light in their community.

When it's all said and done, the actual impact of our discipleship will not be measured in how many dinners we hosted, but in the fruit their marriage bears, long after we're gone. If they go on to disciple another couple, raise God-honoring children, or build a legacy of faith in their own family, that's when we know we've left something eternal. It's not about creating a fan club; it's about building a chain reaction of faith, one couple at a time. And that, my friend, is how legacies are born.

PASSING DOWN FAITH AND MISSION

As godly couples, one of our most significant responsibilities is to be intentional about passing down our faith to others, especially to younger or less experienced couples. Marriage, when lived according to God's design, is a powerful picture of Christ's love for the Church. And while we can certainly enjoy companionship, laughter, and shared goals in our relationship, it's important to remember that our union is not just for our own benefit. It carries a mission, a calling, far bigger than just the two of us.

When we step into the role of mentors, we're not just giving advice or reminiscing about our early years. We're helping another couple anchor their marriage in Christ. We're showing them what it looks like to live out faith daily, to navigate conflict with grace, to love unconditionally even when it's hard, and to serve God together as a team.

But beyond just practical guidance, we point them to their own God-given purpose. God uniquely designs every married couple for a mission. Whether it's raising godly children, serving in ministry, being a light in their workplace, or helping others grow in their faith, their marriage has a divine assignment.

We need to instill in these couples that marriage isn't just about two people finding happiness together. It's about two people joining together to make a spiritual impact. Just as we have a mission from God, they do too. They are not just building a life; they're advancing the Kingdom. And they are called to fulfill that mission with diligence, passion, and obedience to how God is leading them.

When we disciple couples with this mindset, we're not just leaving behind good memories or nice lessons — we're planting purpose. We're calling out the greatness God has placed in them and encouraging them to run their race strong. And when they begin walking in that calling, impacting others the same way, our legacy multiplies far beyond anything we could have imagined. That's the beauty of godly mentorship, it's never just momentary; it's eternal.

LIVING SO YOUR MARRIAGE POINTS TO CHRIST LONG AFTER YOU'RE GONE

One beautiful real-life example is the story of Jim and Elisabeth Elliot, a missionary couple whose lives still echo with the love and mission of Christ long after they have gone.

Jim Elliot felt called to serve God in missions early in life. He was passionate about bringing the gospel to people who had never heard the name of Jesus. In the early 1950s, he and a small group of other young men began planning to reach the Huaorani people (also known as the Auca) — an indigenous tribe in the Ecuadorian rain forest known for their isolated lifestyle and history of violence toward outsiders.

Before setting out on this mission, Jim married Elisabeth Howard. Their courtship and early marriage were deeply rooted in prayer, patience, and a shared sense of purpose. They weren't just in love with each other; they were "on mission" together. Their marriage was marked by prayer, deep faith, and a willingness to sacrifice everything to follow God's call. They knew they were stepping into possible danger, but their commitment to Jesus and to each other remained unshakable.

In 1956, Jim and four other missionaries made contact with the Huaorani tribe after months of preparation. They began a friendly exchange by dropping gifts from a small plane. Eventually, they landed near the tribe in hopes of making face-to-face contact. Tragically, not long after that encounter, all five men were speared to death by the very people they had come to love and serve.

The story could have ended there, a tale of sincere faith cut short, but it didn't. Instead, it became a profound testimony that still points to Christ today.

Elisabeth, just 29 years old at the time, made a decision that shocked the world. Rather than return to the safety and comfort of her homeland, she chose to stay in Ecuador. Incredibly, she and her young daughter later went to live among the very same tribe that had killed her husband. Through grace and forgiveness only possible through Christ, Elisabeth saw hearts change. Many in the tribe, including those responsible for Jim's death, came to faith in Jesus. The Elliots' story became a modern version of the early church's witness, bold, sacrificial, and soaked in the love of Christ.

Elisabeth spent the rest of her life writing, speaking, and discipling others. She authored several books, including her most famous, *Through Gates of Splendor*, which tells the story of Jim and the other missionaries. For decades, her words encouraged countless couples and singles to live with eternal purpose and sacrificial love.

Jim and Elisabeth's marriage lasted less than three years, but its legacy lives on more than half a century later. It wasn't the length of their union that made it powerful — it was its purpose. They lived and loved in such a way that they pointed people to Jesus. Their story is still being told in churches, online, and through mission organizations across the globe.

They remind us that a Christ-centered marriage lived on mission, whether short or long, can spark a movement of faith that ripples far beyond our lifetimes. That's legacy. And it's proof that when two people say yes to God together, there's no limit to what He can do through them.

So what about you? Are you living your marriage in a way that you will be remembered for Christ in eternity? Because here's the truth: our marriages were never meant to be just comfortable partnerships that help us survive life. They were designed with a deeper, eternal purpose. We were built to love one another unconditionally, yes, to support each other, raise children, juggle bills, mow the lawn, and figure out whose turn it is to unload the dishwasher. Still, more than anything, we were created to love Christ even more.

Our marriages should be a loud, everyday testimony of the gospel. They should speak of grace, forgiveness, sacrifice, and mission. God wants to use our marriage not just to bless us, but to impact others for His kingdom. He wants us to pour into other couples, guide younger families, and build a legacy that lasts far beyond the last mortgage payment or the last car ride to soccer practice.

So, the question is: Will your marriage be a pleasant memory for a few or a powerful movement for many? Let's commit to being couples who love each other deeply, serve Christ together faithfully, and invest in others intentionally, so that long after we're gone, our lives still point people to Jesus. That's the kind of legacy worth living for.

MARRIAGE AS A MISSION

What about you? Are you living your life and your marriage in such a way that it will be remembered for Christ into eternity?

Throughout this book, we've explored how God designed marriage not just as a blessing for us to enjoy, but also as a vehicle for advancing His kingdom. From the biblical foundations of oneness and sacrifice to the practical daily acts of love and endurance, we've looked at how marriage shapes us, challenges us, and ultimately equips us to reflect the gospel. But let's not stop at good theory or warm feelings. Now is the time to ask: What will we do with what we've learned?

You see, every marriage tells a story. The question is, what story is yours telling? Is it one of comfort and convenience, or is it filled with courage and calling? Are you building a life together that simply seeks security, or are you leaning into your divine assignment to impact others for Christ? God didn't pair you and your spouse just to make each other happy. He paired you to make heaven crowded.

Marriage is a mission field. Sometimes that field looks like a messy kitchen after dinner, a quiet prayer before bed, or a hard conversation where grace is needed more than a quick comeback. Other times, it looks like inviting another couple into your story, mentoring them through tough times, or joining arms in service to your church or community. Every moment counts. Every decision builds or hinders the legacy you leave behind. One of the most significant marriage goals you can have isn't just to grow old together, but to grow others along the way.

So I ask you: Will your marriage echo into eternity? Will others look at your life and see a love that was rooted in something far deeper than emotion, a love built on mission, surrender, and faith in action?

You won't always get it right, and that's okay. God isn't looking for perfect marriages — He's looking for willing ones. Couples who say, 'God, we're available. Use us.' That availability turns everyday moments into eternal impact. That's the miracle and the mystery of how God works through two imperfect people who are fully yielded to Him.

One day, when you're long gone, and your chairs sit empty at the dinner table, let your marriage still be speaking. Let it testify. Let it stand as a beacon of grace and purpose. Let it be said of you and your spouse: They loved well. They served faithfully. And they lived out their marriage as a mission.

Because in the end, the goal isn't just to be remembered, but to be remembered for pointing others to the only One worth remembering: Jesus Christ.

Marriage as a Mission – Reflection & Action Guide
Reflection Questions

1. Who has invested in your marriage spiritually?
2. How can your marriage impact younger couples or future generations?
3. What legacy of faith do you hope to leave behind?

Mission in Action

- Pray together for a younger couple you could mentor.

- Write down 2-3 intentional ways you want to pass down faith (to kids, grandkids, or spiritual children).
- Take time to celebrate God's faithfulness in your marriage so far by marking it with a special date night, a journal entry, or a testimony shared.

About the Author

About the Author

  Daniel Moore has called Neosho, Missouri, home his whole life. He's been married to his wife, Michelle, for over 20 years, and together they've built a full and busy life with three (now adult) children, two of them who have awesome spouses, two dogs, and now four granddaughters who keep them smiling. Daniel and Michelle co-host the podcast *Marriage Life and More*, where they share weekly conversations about God's design for marriage. Daniel also hosts *Connecting the Gap*, a Bible study podcast that helps listeners dig deeper into Scripture. When he's not working at a Christian radio station or running his computer business, you can usually find him out on a bike ride, kayaking, catching a football game, or just spending time with Michelle — the thing he enjoys most of all!

You can connect with me on:

- https://www.marriagelifeandmore.com
- https://x.com/ctgaponline
- https://www.facebook.com/ctgaponline
- https://www.instagram.com/ctgaponline
- https://www.connectingthegap.net

www.ingramcontent.com/pod-product-compliance
Lightning Source LLC
Chambersburg PA
CBHW061802120626
46550CB00005B/2100